IOWA
AGRICULTURE

IOWA
AGRICULTURE

A History of Farming, Family and Food

DARCY DOUGHERTY MAULSBY
FOREWORD BY SENATOR CHUCK GRASSLEY

AMERICAN PALATE

Published by American Palate
A Division of The History Press
Charleston, SC
www.historypress.com

Cover images: Barn quilts, such as this one near Lake View, have become a common sight in parts of rural Iowa, where they help promote rural tourism and boost economic development. *Author's collection*; roadblocks like this one, organized near Sioux City in 1932 by the Farmers' Holiday Association, protested low prices paid for farmers' products during the desperate days of the Great Depression. *State Historical Society of Iowa, Des Moines*; in 2018, Ames-based Smart Ag made Farm Progress Show history with its autonomous tractor demonstration near Boone. The system runs on AutoCart®, a software application that fully automates a grain cart tractor and can provide farmers with much-needed labor assistance during harvest. *Smart Ag.*

First published 2020

Manufactured in the United States

ISBN 9781467142496

Library of Congress Control Number: 2019956019

Notice: The information in this book is true and complete to the best of our knowledge. It is offered without guarantee on the part of the author or The History Press. The author and The History Press disclaim all liability in connection with the use of this book.

CONTENTS

FOREWORD

As a lifelong farmer who also has worked for six decades representing Iowans in state and federal government, I wear my rural roots as a badge of honor and believe it's important for farmers to have a seat at the policymaking tables. Farmers take the long view of things. Maybe that's why they don't forget important lessons from history.

Only 2 percent of the American population shoulders the responsibility for growing enough food to feed the U.S. population. Our agrarian-based heritage has experienced rapid transformation in the last generation. Fewer Americans, even in Iowa, have a direct link to living or working on a farm. Not enough people appreciate that food security is directly tied to national security. Food security extends beyond national sovereignty. American agriculture—and the farmers, workers and businesses along the supply chain—anchors the U.S. economy and increasingly strengthens U.S. energy independence, as well.

From a historical perspective, there are two rules of thumb I use to explain how important food security is to maintain peace and prosperity in society. Napoleon Bonaparte, emperor of France in the early nineteenth century, reportedly said, "To be effective, an army relies on good and plentiful food." In other words, an army marches on its stomach. Food security ensures that a nation can feed its military, whose men and women in uniform are deployed to protect and defend a nation's sovereignty, at home and abroad. I also like to remind policymakers that any society is only nine meals away from a revolution.

Charles Grassley, farmer and U.S. Senator from Iowa. *Courtesy Charles Grassley.*

Political leaders who embrace the misguided notion that socialism is the answer to peace and prosperity are either grossly misinformed or willfully ignorant about the peril of leaders who promise to fix "inequality" with government control. History teaches us that when government suppresses freedom and liberty, the people's path toward peace and prosperity is replaced with food and medicine shortages, hyperinflation, power outages and even more economic and social inequality. Regimes inspired by utopian socialist principles do not eradicate hunger or poverty; they extinguish peace and prosperity at the expense of individual freedom and liberty.

Despite the regional, ideological and partisan differences that divide Americans, we share a common humanity and fundamental thread of human existence. We all need to eat to survive. Technology and innovation continue to revolutionize farming and food production.

When I started farming in the 1950s, the average corn yield in Iowa was about 45 bushels per acre. Today, Iowa farmers yield an average of 202 bushels per acre. This productivity helps feed and fuel a growing world population with affordable, wholesome food and renewable energy. At the same time, farmers are able to conserve resources and save money using no-till, cover crops and precision agriculture.

With a global population expected to reach nearly 10 billion people by 2050, the importance of agriculture research and education is vital for human civilization. Iowa's deeply rooted agrarian heritage continues to lead the way with excellent opportunities to foster ag literacy; food, plant and animal science; and entrepreneurship.

Iowa boasts a vibrant network of FFA organizations across the state. What's more, Iowa's native son Norman Borlaug paved an agricultural revolution credited with saving 1 billion people from starvation. The Father of the Green Revolution was awarded the Nobel Prize in 1970, and Iowa celebrates his legacy with a statue in the Rotunda of the U.S. Capitol.

Iowa is also home to the World Food Prize. For three decades, it has brought thousands of people from around the world to Des Moines in October to talk about food security in a symposium known as the Borlaug Dialogue.

I'm proud to be among the generations of Iowa farmers who have answered the call to put food on family tables. My son Robin Grassley, a third-generation farmer, and I continue farming 750 acres together.

Checking the rearview mirror to look back at history helps ensure that the road ahead paves the way for prosperity and opportunity for family farmers and all those who earn their livelihoods and enjoy their way of life in rural America. With only 2 percent of the population growing food for the rest of the nation, it's more important than ever to educate consumers about where their food comes from.

—Senator Chuck Grassley,
Iowa

ACKNOWLEDGEMENTS

J ust when you think you're pretty well versed in Iowa's agriculture history, you realize that there's so much more to learn. Undertaking a project as huge as trying to share an overview of Iowa's agricultural history is something I certainly couldn't do alone. I don't pretend that this book even comes close to sharing all the remarkable stories that have shaped Iowa agriculture, but it's a start.

I appreciate the help I received throughout this journey from various museums, libraries, professional historians, agribusinesses, various farm organizations and ag commodity groups, Iowa State University staff, my friends at the State Historical Society of Iowa and farm families across the state. I'm grateful for places that are sharing the story of Iowa agriculture like Living History Farms, the John Deere Tractor & Engine Museum in Waterloo, county museums across Iowa, Heartland Acres Agribition Center in Independence, the Huxley Learning Center, the Heartland Museum in Clarion, the Kossuth County Agriculture & Motorsports Museum in Algona, the Froelich Museum in northeast Iowa and others. Your work matters.

I know I haven't properly thanked everyone who contributed to this book, but rest assured, I do value the resources you've given me that I can share with readers. Finally, I'd like to thank Chad Rhoad and the great team at The History Press for helping bring this book to life and helping preserve Iowa's agricultural history.

ACKNOWLEDGEMENTS

I hope you enjoy this remarkable journey and feel the same sense of awe, amazement and inspiration that I experience each time I explore the rich history of Iowa's agricultural heritage. Let's work together to discover even more possibilities for this dynamic, innovative industry that touches all our lives in countless ways each day.

INTRODUCTION

I t's a beautiful June day in 2019. I'm at a conservation field day on a farm near Grand Junction, Iowa. I'm learning about how Bruce and Jenny Wessling have planted Norway spruce trees, cedar trees and austrees (hybrid willows) near their hog confinement barns to control odor, beautify the farm and help protect the environment not just for today, but for future generations.

It's a warm, sunny morning—the kind that makes me feel so free and so grateful I have the opportunity to experience rural Iowa and its farms firsthand, without being stuck inside an office all day. "If only everyone could see what I get to see every day," I've often thought, especially as I try to do my small part to counter the misinformation that's widespread about modern agriculture.

I wasn't exaggerating when I wrote this description of the field day on my personal Facebook page:

> *Birds singing. Robin eggs in sight. Fresh, clean air. Tree branches swaying gently as a summer breeze drifts by. You might think I'm in a park, but I'm actually just a few feet from some modern hog barns housing a few thousand market hogs in Greene County. It's the "Pork 'N Trees" field day with Trees Forever, and we're standing in a windbreak filled with rows of austrees (hybrid willows), cedar trees, Norway spruce and various shrubs that Bruce and Jenny Wessling planted in 2009.*

The Wesslings were the first farmers in Iowa to participate in the Green Farmstead Partner Program coordinated by the Coalition to Support Iowa's Farmers. Since then, nearly 70,000 trees have been on livestock farms across Iowa, thanks to this eco-friendly program. These windbreaks help control odor (in fact, they reduce odor by 10 to 15 percent, according to Iowa State University data), plus they can help farmers reduce electricity and propane usage at their barns. If that weren't enough, they also help control snow deposition—and they just make a farm look great.

Makes me proud that farmers voluntarily embrace the Green Farmstead Partner Program (farmers aren't required by law to plant these trees). This is a prime example of the power of partnerships and farmers' commitment to the land and the environment.

I've covered hundreds of stories like this since the late 1990s throughout my twenty-plus-year career as an Iowa-based ag journalist and author. I've lived these stories on my own family's Century Farm in Calhoun County, Iowa. I've also learned so much by interviewing hundreds of farmers of all types across Iowa and beyond. I've visited with them in their farm kitchens and shops. I've tagged along to ride with them in their tractors and combines when they're working in the field. I've served with them on the boards of local farm organizations. I've photographed their families, crops and livestock. These are people I know and trust—and I respect them greatly.

That's why a comment from my good friend Duane Murley stuck with me when we were in the Wessling's machine shed, eating lunch after their field day. "Just think about how many ideas that changed the world got started in farm shops and fields like this," said Murley, a longtime farm broadcaster who can be heard over the noon hour every weekday on KWMT in Fort Dodge.

I knew exactly what he meant. We started listing the Iowa ag innovators whose contributions revolutionized farming and food production. Names like Wallace, Borlaug, Carver, Hagie, Sukup, Kinze and more were top of mind. You'll meet them all, and many more fascinating Iowans, in this book.

Yet most people don't get it. Iowa is little more than flyover country to many Americans. It's even easy for many Iowans to feel disconnected from agriculture. The nation counted 3.2 million farmers as of the 2012 Census of Agriculture, or just over 1 percent of the population. Farmers have almost become an endangered species, even here in the heart of farm country.

I always maintain, however, that if you eat, you have a connection to agriculture every day. "If you want to understand Iowa, you need to understand the history of food," said Pamela Riney-Kehrberg, a history professor at Iowa State University. "Throughout the state's history, growing food to feed the nation has been at the center of human activity. Men, women, and children have all contributed to the history of food in Iowa, and food grown in Iowa has fed this state, the nation and the world. In the 'great chain of being,' nothing except air and water is more critical than food, so understanding how it is produced is absolutely essential to having a more complete understanding of our world."

Iowa's often-overlooked history of food and farming is filled with fascinating and often surprising stories and personalities. "The history of Iowa agriculture is a tribute to the generations of men, women and families who worked very hard, overcame extraordinary odds and persevered to make life better—not only for themselves, but for billions of people around the world," said Dr. Wendy Wintersteen, who became the sixteenth president of Iowa State University in 2017.

A basic understanding of farming also puts your definition of agriculture to the test—and that's a good thing, Wintersteen told me. "The breadth and depth of agriculture is extraordinary, touching ordinary people every day, with the food you eat, the water you drink and the air you breathe. A basic understanding of Iowa agriculture can dispel misperceptions and misunderstandings."

All this makes me think of the timeless wisdom of the cowboy poet Baxter Black, whom I met in Ida Grove, Iowa, when he spoke at a farm meeting in 2010. "The list of 'essential professions' is a short one. That's the reality of real life," Black said. "Our culture expends a great deal of effort on future NBA stars, astronauts, environmental lawyers, doctors and political science majors. But for every 100 rock stars, Rhodes Scholars and Heisman trophy winners our country produces, we better make sure we spend enough to train at least two future farmers, so the rest of them can eat."

I couldn't agree more.

Chapter 1

LANDSCAPES THAT SHAPE US

The story of Iowa agriculture begins with the soil. It's one of the most basic resources on which all life depends, it's right beneath our feet and it's one of the most valuable resources we have. Soil is also a silent witness to Iowa's dramatic natural history, influenced through ancient times by shallow seas, violent explosions and huge glaciers. These powerful forces shaped what has become one of the most productive agricultural regions on Earth, yet clues to this land before time endure, recorded in rocks and fossils.

Modern Iowans, both rural and urban, don't have to look far to discover the legacy of Iowa's distant past, which is intertwined with modern life and modern agriculture. In 2017, visitors to the University of Iowa's Mobile Museum got a glimpse of Iowa history that might look like something from a horror movie—a six-foot giant sea scorpion that called Iowa home hundreds of millions of years ago.

Iowa Geological Survey research specialist Paul Liu and his team discovered that a meteorite struck Earth 465 million years ago in the area that is now Decorah in northeast Iowa. In the resulting crater, researchers found an astonishing collection of exceptionally well-preserved fossils. The site represents one of only a few such *lagerstätten* (the scientific term for a fossil deposit of this magnitude) from the Middle Ordovician period, a geologic measure of time when a rich variety of marine life flourished in the vast seas and the first primitive plants began to appear on land.

At that time, a shallow saltwater sea covered much of what is now Iowa and the Midwest. The area around Decorah was near the coast, where the water was

Iowa's fossil record reveals that this six-foot sea scorpion lived in the Decorah area millions of years ago, noted Paul Liu, Iowa Geological Survey researcher. Courtesy *Iowa Geological Survey/University of Iowa.*

less salty. Distinctive organisms evolved to exist in the special conditions there. When the meteorite struck Earth, the water near the crater's seafloor became very still, brackish (slightly salty) and low in oxygen. Organisms in the water died and fell to the seabed, where they were preserved and laid undisturbed until Liu and his colleagues found them. "This opens a new window to tell us what Ordovician life was like," Liu said.

One of the most dramatic finds was the sea scorpion, the earliest and largest such animal of that period, with a long head shield, a narrow curving body and huge, claw-like limbs that could easily trap the creature's unfortunate prey. The sea scorpion's modern relatives include spiders, lobsters and ticks. Imagine a six-foot tick!

FOSSILS PRESERVE IOWA'S ANCIENT HISTORY

As those ancient sea creatures died, their bodies became part of the landscape that would become Iowa. Some became fossils in places like the Devonian Fossil Gorge, which has become a tourist attraction in Iowa City.

This gorge was created by the massive floods of 1993 and was expanded by the flood of 2008, when water topped the emergency spillway. The overflow washed away tons of soil, huge trees and part of the road. When the waters receded, the 375-million-year-old fossilized Devonian ocean floor was revealed.

A similar adventure awaits at the Floyd County Fossil & Prairie Park in northern Iowa, where you can descend 375 million years into what once was a shallow Iowa sea filled with squid, coral and fish-like creatures.

Naturalist Barb McKinstry, who was quoted in the May/June 2007 issue of *Iowa Outdoors* magazine, noted how Iowa's shallow seas millions of years ago were teeming with life, similar to the subtropical islands below the Gulf of Mexico. The ancient fossils that remain today put people's place on Earth into context. "We like people to feel a connection between what is here now, and what this land once was," she said.

Glaciers' Legacy Lives On

While shallow seas and massive meteorites affected Iowa, the icy grip of continental glaciers thousands of years ago remains one of the most significant geologic processes to affect Iowa's agricultural heritage.

Most of the deposits underlying today's land surface are composed of materials known as drift that were moved here by glaciers. The arrival of these glaciers in the state began more than 2 million years ago, and numerous reappearances are recorded in the deposits they left behind.

Among the most famous landforms in Iowa created during the glacial periods are the Loess Hills, a geologic wonder in western Iowa. The Loess Hills are a product of the Illinoian and Wisconsonian glacial periods, when huge quantities of wind-blown silt, or loess (rhymes with "fuss"), accumulated to heights of more than two hundred feet. Although deposits of loess are found in various locations around the world, nowhere else but the Yellow River Valley in China are those deposits higher than they are in Iowa, according to the Loess Hills National Scenic Byway.

Most of the loess deposits occurred between 18,000 and 150,000 years ago, according to historical markers located near the tiny town of Turin along the Loess Hills Scenic Byway. The silt particles that form the Loess Hills were produced by the grinding movement of glaciers on rock underneath. Glacial meltwater carried silt downriver in the summer. In winter, water flowed slowly, and the silt was deposited on the floodplain. Winds picked up soils that had been ground as fine as flour and formed dunes along the ancient waterway that became today's Missouri River.

The process repeated itself during the thousands of years the ice age took to end, enlarging the dunes. Because the prevailing winds were from the northwest, the dunes on the Iowa side of the river were higher than those west of the Missouri. Erosion of the loess soil during thousands of years has helped form the unique landscape that exist today.

To the east of the Loess Hills, landscapes of north-central and west-central Iowa still display the actual shapes that resulted directly from glacial action. This region, known as the Des Moines Lobe, runs from the Minnesota border to Des Moines. It includes the part of the state last touched by the huge sheets of frozen water (the Wisconsin glacier) that invaded Iowa twelve to fourteen thousand years ago.

Archaeologists tell us that this massive glacier was five thousand feet tall—about a mile. It pushed its way south across the Des Moines Lobe from northern Iowa to the area where the state capitol stands in Des Moines at about 0.8 mile per year—a blistering-fast pace for a glacier. Once the glacier got to central Iowa, however, warmer temperatures caused it to melt about twelve thousand years ago.

Landforms of the Des Moines Lobe still retain the distinct imprints of recent glacial occupation, according to *Landforms of Iowa* by Jean C. Prior. As it plowed across the land, pushing rocks and soil with it, the glacier established the present course of the Raccoon River, according to the City of Storm Lake, Iowa. Today, the Iowa portion of the Des Moines Lobe is further outlined by the cities of Clear Lake, Eldora, Carroll, Storm Lake and West Okoboji.

Nearly all of Iowa's natural lakes occur on the Des Moines Lobe. Also, Storm Lake, Lake Okoboji, Spirit Lake, Clear Lake and numerous smaller ponds, sloughs and bogs are characteristic of postglacial landscapes and their sluggish, inefficient drainage networks. When the first settlers came to this part of Iowa, it was said they could travel by boat from Rockwell City to west of Pomeroy in Calhoun County without even taking their boat out of the water.

These wetlands were known for attracting great flocks of nesting and migrating waterfowl, as reflected in the names given to the Des Moines Lobe towns of Mallard and Curlew in Palo Alto County and Plover in Pocahontas County.

Although good for wetland habitat, incomplete surface drainage is a serious impediment to agricultural productivity, Prior noted. Many of the region's native wetlands were drained as agriculture became more important. Glacial erratics, those travel-worn rocks and boulders from regions north of Iowa, are other impediments to agriculture in this area. They generally aren't an issue in the rolling terrain of southern Iowa.

Farmers who must deal with these rocks typically gather them over the years into piles in the corners of fields and on farmsteads, with some ending up as unique garden décor. Clearing fields of rocks and laying drainage tile lines beneath poorly drained areas have turned the Des Moines Lobe into highly productive farmland, Prior noted.

Cultivating a Deeper Understanding of Iowa's Soils

All these factors help explain why Iowa has some of the richest, most productive soil in the world. Most soils in Iowa formed ten to fourteen thousand years ago, after the last glacier in the region melted. Those soils supported the prairies that covered much of Iowa in centuries past. "Understanding the geology of Iowa is important so we can better manage the soils we have today," said Dr. Lee Burras, a professor of agronomy at Iowa State University (ISU) who taught the short course "The Soils of Iowa" during the 2018 Practical Farmers of Iowa's annual meeting in Ames.

Any good farmer knows there's a big distinction between soil and dirt. Soil is one of the most diverse habitats and complex ecosystems on the planet. It's a precious, magnificent resource that holds the secrets to sustainable farming.

Iowa's fertile, black, prairie-derived soils are referred to as mollisols, and they make up more than two-thirds of the state's land base, Burras said. Midwestern mollisols are among the most productive soils in the world, making Iowa a perfect place to grow crops. "One of the reasons that 90 percent of Iowa is farmed is because we have incredible natural soils," Burras said.

Soil is a mixture of sand, silt, clay and an array of microorganisms. Loam is rich soil with roughly equal proportions of sand, silt and clay. "To grow crops, you must start with a loam or silt loam," Burras said. In terms of particle size, sand is the biggest of the three. Silt particles are smaller than flour particles, although the texture of silt feels like flour. Clay particles are the smallest of all and require a microscope to be seen.

Iowa has at least 11,000 different soils and 507 different soil series. "Series" is the local name of soils, such as Clarion, Marshall or Fayette. These series differ based on various soil-forming factors like parent material, time (how long the soil has been forming), climate and biota (the animal and plant life of a particular region, habitat or geological period).

Soil series information stems from soil survey programs that started in the late 1890s in the United States. The first soil survey in Iowa took place in the Dubuque County area, according to ISU Extension. Field work was completed in 1902, and the report was published in 1903.

Beginning in the mid-1960s, Iowa launched an accelerated effort to map soil in all counties in a short time. The agencies involved included the USDA Soil Conservation Service (now the USDA Natural Resources Conservation Service), Iowa Department of Soil Conservation (now Division of Soil Conservation in the Iowa Department of Agriculture and Land Stewardship) and ISU through the Experiment Station and Cooperative Extension Service. Today, all ninety-nine Iowa counties have had multiple soil surveys.

The soil surveys reflect the diverse terrain that has defined Iowa's landscape, from prairies to wetlands to forests to savannahs (a combination of forest and prairie). Soil series determine what grows well in certain areas. Cattails, for example, grown in Harp and Okoboji soils, while big blue stem grass thrives in Clarion and Nicollet soils.

Iowa soils are also defined by the Corn Suitability Rating (CSR) system, which was developed by Iowa State University in 1971 as a way to measure potential soil productivity based on soil profile, slope characteristics and weather conditions. It is an index ranging from 0 to 100, with CSR values of 100 reflecting the most productive soil.

Advances in soil science necessitated an update of the CSR. In 2015, the Corn Suitability Rating 2 (CSR2) was introduced to provide a current index to the inherent productivity of each kind of soil for row-crop production.

Soil productivity is intertwined with soil health. "Soil is the fundamental resource on which human civilization depends," said Dr. David Montgomery, a professor of earth and space sciences at the University of Washington who spoke at the 2019 Iowa Water Conference in Ames. "If you study history, there's a clear connection between degraded soils and impoverished human societies."

It's time to change the way you think about the soil, added Montgomery, the author of *Growing a Revolution: Bringing Our Soil Back to Life*. "How people today treat the land influences how the land will treat future generations."

This public artwork near downtown Conrad in Grundy County celebrates the rich black soil that makes the region's farms so productive. *Author's collection.*

Improved knowledge of the complex relationship between soil and plant roots could bring changes to Iowa agriculture in the next fifteen years that are as vast as the difference between the landline phone and the smartphone, Burras said. Soil links Iowa's past, present and future, he added. "Iowa is a beautiful place with a fascinating history. Once you understand basic geology and its connection to the soil, you can better understand the Iowa we see today."

Chapter 2

IOWA'S FIRST FARMERS

Just as Iowa's soils reveal the history of the state's landscapes, there's evidence of human activity throughout Iowa long before recorded history. I think about my experience at Whiterock Conservancy near Coon Rapids during an archaeological dig that was open to the public in 2018.

Archaeologist Joe Arts passed around a brown stone you could easily hold in your hand. When he started telling the story behind this sandstone, I was hooked. "We've carbon dated a cooking hearth from the area where we found this rock and found that it was about 2,400 years old," said Arts of Iowa City, explaining that the stone we were passing around was fire-cracked rock, which would have been heated to cook food in a pit.

I was stunned by this insight. I became even more excited that I'd chosen to spend my Saturday assisting a team of archaeologists working along the banks of the Middle Raccoon River near Coon Rapids. About ten of us, including professional archaeologists and rank amateurs like me, gathered on a warm, sunny Saturday morning on September 15 to dig into history, literally, at Whiterock Conservancy. This 5,500-acre, nonprofit land trust along seven miles of the Middle Raccoon River Valley balances sustainable agriculture, natural resource protection and public recreation on the landscape.

Whiterock Conservancy began inviting archaeologists to conduct research in the conservancy in 2010 when plans were taking shape to add trails in the area. There have been some remarkable finds in the area since then. Here are five things worth knowing about Iowa's amazing natural history and Native American heritage:

- People have lived in Iowa for thirteen thousand years, with some of the earliest traces of human habitation in areas like Mills County in southwest Iowa that weren't affected by the most recent glacier.
- Agriculture goes back thousands of years in Iowa. Native Americans began farming in Iowa three thousand years ago, noted Cherie Haury-Artz, an archaeologist and education assistant with the Office of the State Archaeologist in Iowa City who joined the Whiterock dig. The development of agriculture and pottery go hand in hand in the archaeological record, she noted. "Also, women were the farmers, while men were hunters and warriors," she added.
- Corn production has defined Iowa for centuries. Corn (maize) was domesticated in Mexico seven thousand years ago, and ancient Iowans began raising it about one thousand years ago, Haury-Artz noted.
- Farming led to villages. Sometimes hundreds or even thousands of people would congregate in permanent villages in Iowa. Earth lodges that have been found in Mills County reflect this, said Haury-Artz, who added that these Native Americans were "big time corn farmers" about one thousand years ago.
- Life was harsh. Living to a ripe old age as a Native American in Iowa hundreds of years ago usually meant living to thirty-five or forty.

There's a remarkable story to be told through the Iowa landscape and the secrets that lie hidden in the soil, Joe Arts said. "There were people here long before us. I view our work as a tribute and a thank-you for letting us learn more of their story."

Meet the Meskwaki

The history of Iowa agriculture also includes the Meskwakis ("Red Earth People"), who were newcomers to the region in the early 1700s. The

Meskwaki nation (officially known as the Sac & Fox Tribe of the Mississippi in Iowa) is the only federally recognized Indian tribe in Iowa today.

"The Sac were more urban and lived in larger villages, while the Fox were more country and lived in smaller groups," said Johnathan Buffalo, historic preservation director for the Meskwaki Nation at Tama, Iowa.

The Meskwakis, who fought against the French in the Fox Wars (1701–42), lived in the St. Lawrence River Valley, Michigan and Wisconsin at various times before moving to the region that would become Iowa, according to the Meskwaki Cultural Center and Museum in Tama. The Meskwakis had resided in Iowa roughly one hundred years before white settlers began moving into the Iowa Territory in the 1830s and early 1840s. The U.S. Dragoons were ordered to the Sac & Fox Agency in 1842. (The First U.S. Dragoons were cavalry soldiers who scouted Iowa in 1835 after the Black Hawk Purchase Treaty of 1832 opened the Iowa Territory for settlement and put the area under U.S. government patrol.)

One reason the Dragoons were ordered to the Sac & Fox Agency was to put down any threatened violence toward the Meskwakis (Sac and Fox). By the early 1840s, the Dragoons had removed numerous trespassers and squatters. The presence of the U.S. Army was not to protect the trespassers from the Indians but to protect the Indians from these trespassers.

In 1842, the tribes signed a removal treaty to Kansas and ceded their lands west of the Mississippi River, including a region in present-day central Iowa. The ceded land was located in present-day central Iowa. Article IV of the treaty created head chiefs for the Sac and Fox tribes. Each head chief was to be paid $500 annually (roughly $15,000 in today's money), according to the Meskwaki Cultural Center and Museum in Tama.

By order of Article III of the Treaty of 1842, the Sac and Fox were to leave Iowa by October 11, 1845, and move to lands in Kansas assigned to them. The treaty's terms allowed for a gradual relocation process of two steps taking place within three years. Theoretically, the first move in 1843 was to be to the western part of the ceded lands past a boundary called the "Painted Rocks" or "Red Rocks." The second move was to cross the Missouri River into Kansas (Osage County and Franklin County) by the 1845 deadline.

In 1843, the Meskwakis assembled at Fort Des Moines on the Raccoon fork of the Des Moines River in preparation to leave the Iowa Territory and cross the Missouri River.

Sac & Fox agent John Beach was extremely displeased to discover that by the early winter of 1845, only one-fifth of the Meskwaki population's whereabouts were accounted for at the Kansas Osage River reservation. Clearly, four-fifths of the Meskwakis were somewhere else—primarily right back in Iowa.

Returning to Iowa

By mid-1845, Beach reported that fewer than 250 of the total 1,271 Meskwakis were at the Kansas reservation. Between 1846 (Iowa became a state on December 28, 1846) and 1852, the Meskwakis continued to range in their former hunting grounds and village sites in Iowa. White settlers complained that the Meskwakis destroyed timber, pulled up stakes and killed game.

Realizing that the white settlers' fears were growing, the Meskwakis sought to create a positive image of themselves, according to exhibits at the Meskwaki Cultural Center and Museum. The Meskwakis lobbied local and state politicians and performed in local community celebrations and special events. They wanted to assure the white population that the mere presence of the Meskwakis was protection against feared tribes like the Sioux in northern Iowa.

Cultivating a New Relationship

Life had been hard for the Meskwakis who moved to the reservation in Kansas. The poor-quality land, such a contrast from the rich Iowa soil, made crops nearly impossible to grow. Diseases such as cholera, smallpox and dysentery flourished in the densely populated reservations. Hunting the dwindling buffalo herds meant increased competition with other Indian tribes confined to nearby reservations.

By the early 1850s, Iowa political leaders had begun working with the Meskwakis to make it legal for them to continue to live in Iowa. The tribe was aided by men like James Berry, an Indiana native who moved to the Iowa Territory in 1838 and became a judge in the Iowa court system by the 1850s. In 1852, Berry led a petition to the U.S. Congress requesting that the Meskwakis be allowed to remain in Iowa.

On June 23, 1852, he wrote, "We take pleasure in saying to the public that those Indians has [*sic*] been in this county for some time and we can

The Meskwaki culture has long included agriculture. By 1857, the Meskwakis had purchased their first eighty acres along the Iowa River in Tama County. *Courtesy of Meskwaki Cultural Center and Museum.*

recommend them as good Sivil Indians and the majority of the citizens of this county have no objection to there [*sic*] remaining in this county and are willing to assist them all they can."

Other supporters included Josiah Bushnell Grinnell, who was elected to the Iowa Senate in 1856. He introduced state legislation that resulted in the passage of a law that allowed the Meskwakis to continue to live in Iowa.

By 1857, the Meskwakis had purchased their first eighty acres along the Iowa River in Tama County. In 1867, the federal government recognized the Meskwaki tribe's residence in Iowa under the name "Sac and Fox of Iowa." The Meskwakis (or *Me skwa ki a ki*), under their federal name "Sac and Fox Tribe of the Mississippi in Iowa," still live on their 7,778-acre settlement in east-central Iowa.

Meskwaki Farming

Meskwaki culture in Iowa has revolved around agriculture for generations, with primary crops including corn, beans and squash.

Corn (*a-ta-mi-ni*) is the main cultivated crop of the Meskwakis. Flint corn, with multicolored blue and red kernels, is the main variety grown, along with a flour corn with blue kernels. The Meskwakis also grow sweet corn.

Traditionally, dried corn was stored in cache pits, baskets and clay pots or wrapped in fiber bags at the tribe's summer houses. Part of the corn would be used at the winter camp or for the return trip in the spring. "We still grow Tama flint corn and use it in soup," said Buffalo, who was born on the Tama settlement in 1954 and grew up speaking the Meskwaki language.

Through the years, Meskwaki gardens also included squash and pumpkins. Both small and large squash varieties have been cultivated. The most common way to prepare squash is to cut it into chunks and cook it in boiling water. It's allowed to boil down until it becomes a pulp. Maple sugar, maple syrup, honey or brown sugar can be added for flavor.

Squash can also be dried and preserved for winter use. Squash can be hung on a string or pole to dry, sliced into rings or cut into strips. "Because our people dried squash to eat, they didn't get scurvy in the winter," Buffalo noted.

Beans were the third staple crop of the Meskwakis. Beans were domesticated long before the arrival of the Europeans. The only bean introduced to the Meskwakis was the lima bean variety in 1891, according to the Meskwaki museum.

Dried beans and dried corn helped extend the food supply into the early spring. Dried beans were often cooked in a soup with pork, chicken or wild game.

Maple Syrup: A Sign of Spring

In the early spring, the Meskwakis traditionally made their "sugar camps" (temporary sites) when leaving their winter camps. There they spent a few weeks making maple syrup, sugar and candy. "Family groups that had dispersed to different camps in the winter met up in the spring to make maple syrup," said Buffalo, who noted that the Meskwakis then returned to their summer villages.

The Meskwakis were historically a semi-nomadic culture, electing to live together in a single, concentrated area during the summer but scattering into smaller, independent areas throughout the winter. The Meskwaki economy combined hunting, gathering and agriculture and did not depend on one source of sustenance exclusively.

Different types of dwellings were used for the different seasonal occupations. After the harvest had been gathered, the Meskwakis left their summer villages and traveled to their hunting grounds, where they broke into small hunting camps.

Since the Meskwakis were not totally dependent on a single way of making a living, they were more flexible in adapting to the sudden, significant changes that devastated so many other tribes that based their community life primarily on agriculture or hunting, noted the Meskwaki Cultural Center and Museum.

ADAPTING TO CHANGING TIMES

Throughout the tribe's history, the Meskwakis managed to blend their traditions with changing circumstances without abandoning their traditional lifestyle. This includes farming methods. "We still have tribe members who farm," Buffalo noted. All this demonstrates a consistent characteristic of the Meskwaki: "The ability to synchronize ancient beliefs and values with ever-changing natural resources and political landscapes in a way that allows the tribe to maintain inherent 'Meskwakiness,'" as noted in an exhibit at the Meskwaki Cultural Center and Museum.

Chapter 3

PIONEER SETTLEMENT AND THE MAKING OF A FARM STATE

It's easy to look at Iowa agriculture today and take for granted all that was required in the 1800s to create thousands of productive farms. Iowa has 55,875 square miles of land. Because this rich land is so ideally suited for farming, more than 85 percent of Iowa's land is used for agriculture, according to the Iowa Department of Agriculture and Land Stewardship.

Today, Iowa has roughly 87,000 farms and 129,000 farm operators, according to the Iowa Farm Bureau Federation. More than 97 percent of these Iowa farms are owned by families. In 2016, Iowa ranked second in the nation in farm cash receipts at $26.5 billion.

The roots of these modern achievements go back more than two hundred years to the Louisiana Purchase of 1803. Wars and financial difficulties prompted the French military and political leader Napoleon Bonaparte to sell the Louisiana Territory for $15 million to the United States. President Thomas Jefferson purchased nearly 828,000 square miles of land west of the Mississippi River to the Rocky Mountains. The Louisiana Purchase nearly doubled the size of the United States.

It was the real estate deal of the nineteenth century, as the massive territory was purchased for less than three cents per acre. Part or all of nearly fifteen states would be created from the Louisiana Purchase, including Iowa, but first the boundaries of the newly acquired territory had to be determined. Jefferson commissioned Captain Meriwether Lewis and Lieutenant William Clark to lead the Corps of Discovery into the vast northwest regions of the Louisiana Purchase, with the first leg of the journey along the Missouri River along what would become Iowa.

Following the Louisiana Purchase, the region that would become the state of Iowa on December 28, 1846, was under the jurisdiction of various territories, starting with the Louisiana Territory in 1805, the Missouri Territory in 1812, the Michigan Territory in 1834 and the Wisconsin Territory in 1836. As more settlers moved west and the population grew, the region that would become Iowa began to gain its own identity, along with a reputation for fine farmland. By the summer of 1838, the U.S. Congress had approved the creation of the territory of Iowa. Robert Lucas was appointed the first territorial governor.

The First Legislative Assembly convened at Burlington on November 12, 1838. Burlington remained the seat of the territorial government until the Fourth Legislative Assembly, which convened at Iowa City on December 6, 1841. Iowa City remained the capital of the Iowa Territory (and later the state after Iowa achieved statehood on December 28, 1846) for a short time until Des Moines was designated Iowa's capital city in 1857.

This period of Iowa history set in motion events that still affect Iowans' lives, starting with the boundaries that define the counties and townships. Look at any map of Iowa; the names of the counties, townships and towns offer a fascinating reflection of mid-1800s Iowa history and American history itself. There are Native American names (including towns like Oskaloosa and Pocahontas and counties like Pottawattamie and Mahaska), counties named after battles in the Mexican-American War in the 1840s (Cerro Gordo and Buena Vista) and counties named after national political leaders like President James K. Polk and George M. Dallas, vice president in the Polk administration.

THE KEY ROLE OF THE SURVEYOR

Names are just part of the story of Iowa's counties, townships and towns. Look around any Iowa community. Imagine how things looked before human settlement. Consider what it was like to be one of the first to plan and map what we see today.

Surveyors played an integral role in this process. Surveying is the work of examining, measuring and recording the area and features of a piece of land, usually to construct a map or to plan a building or town. America's first president, George Washington, was an avid land surveyor throughout his life.

Surveyors played a vital role in Iowa's settlement. James McClure became Calhoun County's first county engineer in 1872. McClure surveyed the entire county, likely on horseback, as there were few roads at the time. *Courtesy of Stan McClure.*

Surveying in Iowa began in the early 1800s even before Iowa was a state. By the time Iowa was being settled extensively in the mid-1800s, the role of the land surveyor had become extremely important. Surveyors plotted out state and county borders, surveyed land parcels so the U.S. government could sell the property to settlers and helped to lay out new towns.

By the middle of the 1800s, much of the state had been surveyed, creating counties, townships and sections. Iowa today has ninety-nine counties. So, what are townships and sections? Loosely defined, if you lay out a grid over the map of Iowa with one mile in between every line, the square miles created are called sections. This grid was part of a national surveying plan developed in America's infancy. The Land Ordinance Act of 1785 created this rectangular survey system to help establish landownership boundaries.

Counties in Iowa contain townships. Typically, a township is a six-by-six-mile square. Each township is divided into thirty-six sections (each section is a square mile). While the townships are named, each section within a township is numbered.

Each section of a township contains 640 acres. This helps explain why the average farm size in Iowa in the early 1900s was 160 acres, as each section split nicely into four farms of manageable size for the technology available to most farmers of the time.

If you've ever wondered where the phrase "the back 40" comes from, note that each individual section of land can be divided evenly into four 160-acre chunks called quarter sections. So "the back 40" refers to the farthest 40-acre quarter-quarter section of the farm.

Plat maps of Iowa's counties show township divisions and numbered sections. Plat maps also reflect changes in land ownership. Farm families who live on the land generation after generation often feel a strong sense of place in their township, similar to the way urban residents can feel a connection to their neighborhood.

BREAKING NEW GROUND

As settlers moved into the new counties and townships created across Iowa, the pioneers preferred areas with timber. Trees provided material to build log cabins. Timber also supplied a vital fuel source for hearth fires that supplied heat for cooking and warmth. Those first homes on the Iowa frontier were tiny by today's standards, but they provided much-needed shelter. After the Gaylord family of Illinois arrived in Fremont County in southwest Iowa in 1846, the father "built a rude log cabin, 16 feet by 16 feet, with puncheon floor, clay fireplace and mud-and-stick chimney," noted Allan Bogue in his book *From Prairie to Corn Belt*.

Timber was also used to build rail fences. "The axe, the maul and the wedges were more often in the hands of the settler prior to the mid-1850s than were the plow handles or the cradle [implement for cutting grain]," Bogue wrote. One pioneer who arrived in Davis County in southeastern Iowa during the 1840s estimated that he had made more than 150,000 rails for the people of Fox River Township.

The vast expanses of rolling prairie that covered much of Iowa were often compared to vast oceans of meadowland. Diverse plant life included native, blooming flowers that danced among the tall grasses. Wild strawberries and plums could also be found in wild abundance, according to early explorers' reports.

For travelers like William Ferguson, writing in *America by River and Rail*, published in 1856, "the feeling of relief with which one escapes from the interminable forests of the middle states into these boundless 'earth oceans' becomes changed almost to oppression, as you gaze upon the expanse of grass."

Others took a different view. "The gaiety of the prairie, its embellishments, and the absence of the gloom and savage wilderness of the forest, all contributed to dispel the feeling of loneliness which usually creeps over the mind of the solitary traveler in the wilderness," noted N. Howe Parker in *Iowa as It Was in 1855*.

In any case, as the pioneers began to settle in frontier Iowa and create farms, the first step (right along with building shelter in the form of a sod house or log cabin) was to prepare land that would become a field. The thickly interwoven roots of the prairie grasses were especially tough in the marshier areas. "Such sod defied the conventional plows of the settlers," Bogue noted. Local blacksmiths met the challenge by building special prairie-breaking plows, the largest of which could turn a furrow of some thirty inches. "For such work, five or six yokes of oxen, or four horses, might draw the plow, and, with the oxen, at least, two men were required, one to drive the team and the other to guide the plow and regulate the depth of the furrow," Bogue wrote.

Depending on the width of the furrow turned by the plow and the nature of the vegetation, the prairie breakers could turn one and a half to three

As the pioneers began to settle in frontier Iowa and create farms, one of the first steps was to prepare land that would become a field. These men are breaking the prairie in Sioux County around 1890. *Courtesy of City of Ireton.*

acres of sod per day, with frequent stops along the way to file and sharpen the cutting edge of the plowshare.

Prairie-breaking on this scale required an investment in special machinery and livestock that many settlers were not prepared to make. Instead, they hired custom prairie breakers, men who maintained plows and teams for this specialized work. Many young men amassed the funds needed to start their own farms by working behind the breaking plow, Bogue said.

The farmer who hired his prairie breaking done paid $2 to $4 per acre for this service (roughly $65 to $130 per acre today). Those who turned to the professional breakers usually couldn't afford to have more than a few acres broken each year. Many settlers broke their land in a much humbler fashion. It was a slow process, as prairie breaking season lasted only a few months and overlapped the period when the corn crop demanded attention.

"Prairie breaking is going on in every direction," a pioneer named T.M. Ewing in Adair County near Fontanelle wrote in 1869, as recorded by the *Adair County Register*. "We break with every kind of team, from two horses up to the heavy team of six yoke of oxen. We use every sized plow, from 12 to 30 inches."

The invention of the steel plow was nothing short of revolutionary for pioneer farmers in the Midwest. The implement dates back to 1837, when Illinois resident John Deere was just a typical blacksmith turning out hayforks, horseshoes and other essentials for life on the prairie.

Then one day, a broken steel sawmill blade gave Deere an opportunity. He knew well the backbreaking work famers experienced near his home in Grand Detour, Illinois. While plowing, they often interrupted their work to scrape the sticky prairie soil from their cast-iron plows. Deere envisioned a "self-scouring" system where soil would slide easily off of a highly polished, steel moldboard. With steel scarce in the area, Deere acquired a broken steel saw blade and used it to craft a new type of moldboard plow. Now, nearly two centuries later, the company that grew out Deere's success with this innovative plow continues to manufacture advanced farming equipment.

Back in the mid-1800s, however, modern farming technology like the steel plow was just the first step to carving a farm from the prairie. "With the act of breaking, the farm-maker crossed a great divide," Bogue added. "Until that point, his land was an investment, perhaps even a home; now it became a farm."

Grain Mills Grew When Wheat Was King in Iowa

When farm families began moving into southeastern Iowa and along the Mississippi River in the 1830s and 1840s, they grew most of their own food, as well as feed for their livestock. Wheat was often regarded as a cash crop that could be sold to mills and processed into flour.

Being able to supply basic needs like flour depended on home-grown resources in those pioneer days, since the railroad transportation and connections to eastern markets were rudimentary at best or nonexistent in many parts of Iowa. While railroad transportation came to Iowa in the late 1840s, according to the Iowa Department of Transportation, Iowa had only about 655 miles of track in operation by 1860.

Grain mills could be found all over Iowa by the mid-1800s. In fact, Iowa once boasted about seven hundred mills, according to the Northeast Iowa Tourism Association. By the mid-1800s, Iowa had also become one of the biggest wheat-producing states in the nation.

After Iowa wheat production reached its peak in 1875, Iowa's mills started fading away by the 1880s. Grasshopper plagues of almost biblical proportions decimated Iowa farmers' wheat crops periodically in the late

1860s into the 1870s, especially in the north-central and northwest parts of the state. Farmers began shifting from wheat to corn production and never looked back.

The development of the railroads also made Iowa's small towns and farms less dependent on flour and other staples from locally operated, family-run mills, since trains could deliver a wider variety of affordable products from distant locations. Iowa had approximately 9,200 miles of railroad track by 1900, a number that peaked between 1911 and 1917, when more than 10,500 miles of track crisscrossed Iowa, according to the Iowa Department of Transportation.

Through all these changes, however, Cedar Rapids remained a grain milling hub in Iowa. In 1873, the North Star Oatmeal Company decided to open an oatmeal mill in Cedar Rapids, according to the Iowa Pathways project from Iowa Public Television. Other grain milling companies thrived in Cedar Rapids through the years, including the Douglas Starch Works. Founded in 1903 by George Douglas and his brother, Walter, the Douglas Starch Works produced cooking starch and oil, laundry starch, animal feed, soap stock and industrial starches from corn.

Grain milling remains an essential industry in Cedar Rapids today. In 2017, the *Cedar Rapids Gazette* ran the story "Cargill Marks 50 Years of Cedar Rapids Corn Mill," noting the dramatic growth of the operation. "When it was just starting, the corn milling plant on Cedar Rapids' southeast side processed just 9,000 bushels of corn a day—about 40 football fields. Five decades later, the Cargill Corn Milling plant goes through 100,000 bushels a day."

FARMER BECAME UNDERGROUND RAILROAD CONDUCTOR

Establishing farms and homesteads on the Iowa frontier often involved hardship and danger. Sometimes the danger came more from legal and political threats rather than economic forces or Mother Nature.

While slave ownership was never legal in Iowa, freedom seekers traveled through the state in the 1850s via the Underground Railroad, which ran across the southern and central regions of Iowa. This network of secret routes and safe houses passed through the property of pioneer farmer James Cunningham Jordan (1813–1891) and his wife, Melinda, who were some of the earliest settlers in Polk County's Walnut Township.

James Jordan was born in 1813 in what is now West Virginia in a community where slavery was ingrained in the culture. Jordan, a cattle farmer, was expected to assist family members and neighbors in their hunt for escaped slaves. Jordan's branch of the family, however, was influenced by a religious movement called the Second Great Awakening, a Protestant revival that opposed slavery and swept the country by the early 1800s. These experiences fueled Jordan's abolitionist zeal, especially as he moved westward.

After Jordan settled in Polk County in Walnut Township, he chose a beautiful location with ancient oak, walnut and hickory trees on land gently sloping to the Raccoon River. Jordan's first shelter was a lean-to tent, which he replaced in 1848 with a log cabin. In 1850, Jordan and his wife began work on the first phase of a new frame house.

Jordan became a successful farmer, livestock dealer and bank director. Although Jordan's dream was to develop and manage a financially successful livestock business, he remained deeply committed to helping others achieve their dreams as well. He supported the Methodist Episcopal Church and belonged to the new Republican Party, which included many members who opposed the Kansas-Nebraska Act, which Congress passed in 1854.

The Kansas-Nebraska Act allowed people in the territories of Kansas and Nebraska to decide for themselves whether to allow slavery within their borders. The act repealed the Missouri Compromise of 1820, which prohibited slavery north of latitude 36°30'. The Kansas-Nebraska Act infuriated many in the North, who considered the Missouri Compromise to be a long-standing, binding agreement. There was strong support for the Kansas-Nebraska Act, however, in the proslavery South.

Proslavery and antislavery supporters rushed in to settle Kansas and affect the outcome of the first election held there after the law went into effect. Violence soon erupted, with the antislavery forces led by the radical abolitionist John Brown. The territory earned the nickname "Bleeding Kansas" as the death toll rose.

Back in Iowa, many citizens wanted to avoid involvement in the slavery issue and keep black settlement out of the state altogether, while others saw Iowa standing strong as a beacon of freedom and opportunity for all. When Jordan was elected to the Iowa Senate in the mid-1850s, he and his colleagues in the state legislature helped the Meskwaki Indians regain the land they had lost in Iowa after being relocated to Kansas in the mid-1840s.

While Jordan was described as a quiet, modest man who was widely known for the kindness and generosity, he despised slavery and spoke

James Jordan, a pioneer farmer in the area that would become West Des Moines, was the chief conductor of the Underground Railroad in Polk County. *Author's collection.*

out vehemently against it. Jordan was actively engaged in the abolitionist movement, becoming the chief conductor of the Underground Railroad in Polk County. Jordan knew this involvement in the Underground Railroad was dangerous and illegal. Nevertheless, he sheltered fugitive slaves on his Walnut Township farm.

At the state level, Jordan promoted the antislavery Republican Party, and on the national level, he befriended the radical abolitionist John Brown. Brown stayed at the Jordan farm (which is now the Jordan House Museum at 2001 Fuller Road in West Des Moines) at least twice, the last time in 1859, when he was leading a group of slaves he had recently liberated in Missouri to freedom in Canada, according to the West Des Moines Historical Society.

On February 17, 1859, Brown led twelve men, women and children who had been enslaved in western Missouri to the Jordan homestead. The small group had begun their journey at a rural Iowa hamlet known as Civil Bend, an Underground Railroad stop just upriver from Nebraska City, Nebraska. From there, Brown brought the refugees a bit closer to emancipation. As they neared central Iowa, the group rested in a stand of timber near the Jordan farm.

The freedom seekers traveled the next day to a place called Hawley's farm east of Des Moines. Their three-month journey took them to Grinnell, Iowa City and eventually Detroit, Michigan. In the late summer of 1859, the group ferried across the Detroit River to freedom in Windsor, Canada.

Just a few months later, on October 16, 1859, John Brown and an eighteen-man "army of liberation" raided the federal arsenal at Harpers Ferry, West Virginia, hoping to seize a supply of weapons and spark a rebellion of slaves. Brown was subsequently captured, found guilty of treason and hanged on December 2, 1859.

Jordan's role in the Underground Railroad has been honored for generations. *The History of Polk County*, published in 1880, stated that "Jordan has been a life-long enemy of slavery; his devotion to the political life as a staunch and stalwart Republican is the outgrowth of deep-seated conviction; it is among the pleasant things to remember, that under his protecting roof John Brown and his associates, with more than a score of recently liberated slaves, have offered their prayers and sung their first jubilee hymns on their way to Canada."

Today, the Jordan House, a stately Victorian home of Italianate Gothic design, is one of the oldest structures in Polk Country and is one of the few locations in Iowa where visitors can tour the home of an Underground Railroad conductor. The home is listed on the National Register of Historic Places and is part of the National Underground Railroad Network to Freedom Program.

Perhaps Jordan's legacy was best summarized by Jordan's pastor, who eulogized him by stating, "In the troublous days of slavery this great heart reached out and helped the oppressed, seeking the north star of freedom."

Chapter 4

GROWING IOWA'S FARMS AND TOWNS

O n the eve of the Civil War, much of Iowa remained on the frontier. The next forty years would bring sweeping changes that would transform all of Iowa into a thriving network productive farms, small towns and growing cities. First, however, Iowans would play many key roles in the Civil War, which broke out in April 1861.

During the Civil War, seventy-six thousand Iowa soldiers served their state and nation, according to the Iowa National Guard. In relation to its population, Iowa sent more soldiers to the Civil War than any other state.

On the homefront, sheep production showed the most rapid rise and decline of any sector of Iowa agriculture during the 1860s. During the war, wool was in high demand from the U.S. Army, both for military uniforms and blankets. The supply of cotton from the South had been cut off, so a substitute was needed for that material. A bulky commodity like wool could be shipped to the eastern United States much more affordably than other ag commodities.

In 1860, Iowa farmers raised 258,228 sheep and clipped 660,858 pounds of wool. By 1865 (the year the Civil War ended), the number of sheep in Iowa had skyrocketed to more than 1 million, with a wool yield of more than 2.8 million pounds. A combination of affordable farmland, low labor requirements, high prices paid for wool, cheap corn and a good climate for livestock production made Iowa an ideal place to expand the sheep industry. "No state east of the Rocky Mountains, in the same latitude, can produce wool cheaper," observed the editor of the *Country Gentleman* magazine.

The State of Iowa also helped foster the growth of the sheep industry during this period. Governor Samuel Kirkwood proposed a five-year tax exemption on flocks of fifty sheep or smaller. Further tax exemptions were earmarked for capital invested in Iowa's woolen mills. Entrepreneurs like Joseph Shields in Davenport established woolen mills in Iowa to meet this wartime demand.

This intense interest in sheep only lasted for the duration of the Civil War. By 1868, fewer than half of the thirty Iowa counties reporting to the Iowa Agricultural Society mentioned sheep production, and only six (Appanoose, Adams, Harrison, Marion, Mitchell and Van Buren) gave a favorable report, according to Leila Mae Bassett of Iowa State College in her 1933 thesis "Agricultural Experiments in Iowa During the Civil War Decade."

Railroads Speed the Settlement of Iowa

While sheep production dwindled in Iowa in the post–Civil War period, this era ushered in a tremendous railroad boom. A rapidly growing network of rail lines across Iowa made it simpler for more settlers to move to Iowa and easier for Iowa farmers to ship their products to market.

Railroad transportation had arrived in Iowa as early as the late 1840s. Although there were several very small railroads operating in and around Iowa river towns, the first railroad to cross the Mississippi River was the Mississippi and Missouri Railroad in 1856, according to the Iowa Department of Transportation.

While Iowa had only approximately 655 miles of track in operation by 1860, on the eve of the Civil War, this jumped to 2,683 miles by 1870 and nearly tripled to almost 9,200 at the turn of the twentieth century. The miles of track in Iowa peaked between 1911 and 1917 with more than 10,500 roadway miles of track, according to the Iowa Department of Transportation.

Before the coming of the railroads, transportation in Iowa was primarily dependent on the Mississippi River and its tributaries. Wagon transportation was so inadequate that overland routes were used no more than the internal trade of the state required, Bassett said.

Saying that Iowa's roads were unsatisfactory was an understatement. During periods of rain or snow, they became virtually impassable. In 1856, Congress made its first grant to Iowa to aid in railroad construction, Bassett

Crews are shown building a new railroad to Lohrville, which once boasted three rail lines. Expansion of the railroads following the Civil War accelerated the settlement of Iowa. *Courtesy of Toni Kerns.*

said. "The grant composed every alternate section for six sections in width on each side of four proposed railroads extending from the Mississippi to the Missouri. Railroads so aided were to be retained for national use, free from toll or charge for transporting property or troops, and were to carry mail on such terms as Congress designated."

THE GREAT LAND-GRANT HUNT: HOW IOWA FARMLAND HELPED FINANCE IOWA STATE

The federal government's involvement in Iowa's development in the 1860s and beyond wasn't limited to railroads. The story of how more than 200,000 acres of prime Iowa farmland helped finance the beginnings of Iowa State College (now Iowa State University) has been called a great treasure hunt as more Iowa landowners discover their connection to this unique history.

Iowa State University (ISU) is the first land-grant university to identify and map the parcels that the federal government gave to states under the Morrill Act of 1862. States receiving the federal gift had to promise to use the proceeds of the sale of that land to build "people's colleges," where working-class students could get both a practical science and liberal arts education. In Iowa, this opportunity spurred the growth of Iowa State College in Story County.

Contrary to common belief, not a single acre of Story County land was given to Iowa State as part of the Morrill Act. Instead, the public lands that helped grow a small ag college in Ames into a major university were scattered throughout northwest Iowa. Webster, Calhoun, Kossuth, Palo Alto, Emmet, Clay and others—twenty-seven counties in all, according to ISU.

"This land could be leased or sold," said Ray Hansen with Iowa State University Extension, who noted that the average sale price for this prime land was two to four dollars per acre. "The land-grant process set Iowa up for success."

Iowa: A Home for Immigrants

Land grants weren't the only enticement attracting settlers to Iowa 150 years ago. In 1870, the Iowa Board of Immigration in Des Moines published *Iowa: The Home for Immigrants*. This ninety-six-page guide was printed in English, German, Norwegian, Swedish and Dutch and was widely distributed. The Board of Immigration sent twenty thousand pamphlets, along with several representatives, to New England and the mid-Atlantic states to promote settlement in Iowa.

The brochure emphasized, "There is still in Iowa uncultivated land enough for 360,000 farms of 80 acres each." The guide also mentioned that there were still 250,000 acres of government land available for homesteading in northwest Iowa. (The Homestead Act, which President Abraham Lincoln signed into law on May 20, 1862, granted up to 160 acres of government-surveyed, public land to any adult U.S. citizen or intended citizen who occupied it for five years and made improvements to the parcel. It also allowed settlers to purchase the acreage outright at $1.25 per acre after six months of residence.)

Filled with lofty prose, the guide touted Iowa's agricultural bounty and boundless opportunities for new farmers: "Iowa is peculiarly an agricultural state. Whatever inducements she may at present, or in the future, offer to the manufacturer, the miner or persons engaged in the various other pursuits of life, the essential fact remains that the true source of her rising greatness and prospective grandeur lies in the capacity of her soil to supply those staples absolutely necessary for the sustenance of man."

The brochure also highlighted the wide variety of crops that could be grown in Iowa, including corn. It noted that under favorable circumstances, corn yielded 50 to 100 bushels per acre. "In 1867, Iowa produced about 70 million bushels of corn in 1867 and more than 76.5 million bushels by 1868," the brochure noted. "This crop, as well as all others, is raised with less than half the labor usually required on the worn-out soils, or among the stones and stumps, with which the eastern farmer has to contend."

While wheat had also been a leading crop in Iowa up to this point, it didn't get nearly as much press in the brochure as corn. Wheat was lumped into the brochure's short section on small grains. "Our soil is well adapted to the production of buckwheat, barley and rye, though our farmers have not given them so much attention as they have other crops."

BRITISH INVASION AT LE MARS
PLANTED GENTLEMAN ON THE PRAIRIE

This new era of Iowa agriculture attracted immigrants from many parts of western Europe. While the northwest Iowa town of Le Mars, for example, could attribute its growth to German, Irish, Scottish, Welsh and Dutch immigrants, a distinctive British influence marked one of the most unique chapters of Iowa's ag history and settlement in the 1800s.

"They descend from the recesses of the Pullman palace cars dressed in the latest London and Paris styles, with Oxford hats, bright linen shining on their bosoms, a gold repeater ticking in the depths of their fashionably cut vest pockets, and probably carrying the latest agony in canes," according to the *Le Mars Sentinel*, as it described the scene at the railroad depot in April 1881. The story added that the English arrivals unloaded "box after box, trunk after trunk, until a miniature mountain has been built on the platform." One family arrived with eighty-two pieces of luggage!

The story of the English colony in northwest Iowa began in Philadelphia in 1876. Cambridge-educated William B. Close from England and Daniel Paullin, a land agent who was promoting land sales in Illinois and Iowa, visited about the investment opportunities Iowa offered. Inspired by Paullin's idea, Close conceived the notion that he could make money as a land speculator in fertile northwestern Iowa. He persuaded his brothers, Frederick and James,

The Close brothers from England, including John (*left*) and William, saw an opportunity to encourage sons of the British aristocracy to become landed gentry on the prairies near Le Mars. *Courtesy of City of Le Mars.*

to join the venture, and they organized the Iowa Land Company and opened their first land office in Le Mars in February 1879.

The Close brothers, especially William, weren't interested in the hard work of farming. They wanted to transplant English aristocracy to a self-contained colony, where they could live the life to which they were accustomed, noted the July 7, 1986 Associated Press article "In Prairie Settlement, Cricket Matches and Tributes to the Queen."

The Close family was well connected socially and financially in England and managed to secure solid financing for their venture. The Closes encouraged upper-class Englishmen to join the colony. It wasn't as hard a sell as it might seem, since only firstborn sons inherited titles. For other sons, crossing the ocean to become landed gentry on the prairies of fertile Iowa seemed like a good proposition.

Through fancy advertising and some good luck, the idea caught on. Well-heeled Brits came to northwest Iowa to buy farms and set up banks and other businesses. Le Mars became the center of an English colony that spread through several counties. Meanwhile, immigrant farmers from other lands, along with native-born Americans who were living in the area and trying to get by as best they could on their farms, looked on in amazement and amusement.

The Close Colony even provided schools for "pups," those younger sons of English aristocracy who had been encouraged to travel to Le Mars to learn the business of farm management. While the pups worked, the land owners of the Close Colony congregated at the Prairie Club, an exclusive place modeled after a London club, complete with imported liquor, newspapers and magazines from England and traditional English cooking. (In the early years, Americans were not allowed at the club, although this rule was relaxed in later years.)

In addition, the Englishmen met at taverns called the House of Lords and the House of Commons in downtown Le Mars. They also organized other sporting events and social events to entertain themselves, including horse racing, polo matches, cricket matches, dances, steeple chasing, toboggan sledding and fox hunting with hounds. The pups didn't seem to take farm management very seriously either. They were sometimes known to unhitch plow horses for informal racing and betting.

By the 1880s, Le Mars had become the most well-known city in America, other than New York City and Chicago, among the British people, according to the City of Le Mars. By the 1890s, however, the English colony was dying. Many Englishmen came to Iowa, made money on their land and returned home. Others couldn't take the weather and cultural differences. Some married Americans and integrated into local society.

The Close Colony faltered after Frederick Close died in a polo accident in 1890, the same year that marked the beginning of an economic depression that reached its peak in 1893, lowering land values and turning most agriculture unprofitable, according to the book *Gentlemen on the Prairie* by Curtis Harnack, who grew up in Plymouth County near Le Mars.

These woes were only compounded when William was in England going through an ugly divorce, and a fire destroyed the Prairie Club in 1895. Little remains today of the British flair the Close Colony brought to the prairies of northwest Iowa.

Still, the legacy of the Close Colony stands out in Iowa's agricultural history. "The settlers in the Close Colony felt they could do anything because they were gentlemen and British," Harnack wrote. "It was a faith that took them far."

Chapter 5

BONANZA FARMING, IOWA-STYLE

L iving large on the Iowa prairies in the late 1800s wasn't limited to English elites. At one time, Sac County in western Iowa boasted two bonanza farms, Brookmont Farm and the Adams Ranch, that covered thousands of acres each in the Odebolt area.

In the nineteenth century, bonanza farms were found primarily in Minnesota and North Dakota, particularly in the Red River Valley. These massive farms covered thousands of acres and produced large wheat crops. Absentee landowners hired local managers to run the farms. Between 1875 and 1890, bonanza farms became highly profitable through the use of new machinery and huge crews of cheap hired labor. Over time, the land was exhausted, and the great farms were no longer profitable. The investors sold or rented the land to smaller farmers until, by the 1920s, the last remnants of the bonanza period had faded away.

The bonanza farms of Sac County shared some similarities to those operations, yet there were many major differences. Why did these farms develop in Sac County? In the mid-1800s, the federal government gave land grants to railroads to help them build tracks across Iowa and beyond. The rapid settlement in Iowa concentrated the railroad land grants in this part of western Iowa by the early 1870s. Thousands of acres of land were available at a minimal cost—a tempting opportunity for settlers and investors.

The Cook Ranch, officially known as Brookmont Farm, was located north of Odebolt and got its start in the early 1870s, all for five dollars per acre. "In 1873, Charles W. Cook of Chicago bought 12 square miles

(7,680 acres) in what are now Cook Township and Richland Township in Sac County," noted Dan and Don Etler, who shared this history during a program in Odebolt in 2014. "It was the largest contiguous farm in the history of Iowa."

The Cook family, who had settled in Chicago in 1853, made their fortune through their stone quarry business. Their company thrived during the building boom that followed the Great Chicago Fire of 1871.

Charles Willard (C.W.) Cook, one of the sons of this family, became a business success in his own right and would become the link to farmland in Sac County, Iowa. Two of his business associates, Hiram Wheeler and Marvin Hughitt, told Cook about large parcels of railroad land being sold in western Iowa, noting that land could be a great investment.

On April 15, 1873, Cook purchased twelve square miles of prime western Iowa land that would become Brookmont Farm. He paid $5 an acre, for a total of $38,400. This would have equated to $700,000 in current dollars.

Why did Cook choose this particular area? The railroad likely played a role, Dan Etler noted. An Andreas Atlas from 1875 showed a proposed Iowa Pacific Railroad line that was planned to run between Sac City and Ida Grove, right through the area that would become Brookmont Farm. "The potential of a future railroad—one that ultimately was never built—influenced Cook's decision to purchase land in this area," Dan Etler said.

The former Wheeler Ranch (also known as Fairview Farm and later the Adams Ranch) covered more than 6,400 acres in Sac County, making it one of the largest farms in Iowa by the early 1900s. *Author's collection.*

Now an Iowa landowner, Cook began making plans for a large grain and cattle farm based on the tenant model. The operation would include twenty-three sub-farms (half sections of land), plus a central plant and residence. The first farm manager at Brookmont was Jacob Anderson from Illinois, whom Cook met in the Chicago area. The first six to seven years at Brookmont were spent developing the farm. The Cook family, however, stayed in Chicago for most of the 1870s.

Anderson was responsible for the tree-lined roads that were a signature of Brookmont Farm. These trees were predominantly cottonwoods that had been dug from the Missouri River bottoms south of Sioux City and hauled overland to Sac County. The trees were planted in double rows around each section of land. Windbreaks were also planted on all tenant sites. "We estimate there would have been about sixty thousand trees," Dan Etler said. "What an amazing undertaking that was."

As Brookmont Farm developed, it became a small community in itself, with multiple homes, a carriage house, a water tower, a fifty-foot-tall granary for grinding and mixing feed, a two-hundred-foot-long machinery hall, a central office and a two-hundred-foot corncrib that could hold 150,000 bushels of corn.

Brookmont Farm's first mansion, which was likely built between 1879 and 1882, was truly a "palace of the prairie," complete with gas lighting and running water. The Cooks typically lived at Brookmont only during the growing season, arriving in May and leaving in October, Dan Etler noted. They spent their winters in California at Coronado Island, in Chicago or traveling abroad.

Imported Hereford Cattle Arrive at Brookmont Farm

By the early 1880s, however, C.W. Cook had gotten serious about his farm. In June 1883, he traveled to Herefordshire, England, where he selected 306 Herefords, including 296 heifers and 10 bulls, from four prominent cattle breeders. He paid a staggering $200,000 for his new livestock. This would equate to more than $5 million today.

Cook and the cattle traveled by train to the port city of Liverpool, England, where they boarded the chartered ship *Quebec* for an eleven-day trip to North America. The cattle were quarantined in Canada for three months. On September 30, 1883, a dedicated train of twenty-three cattle cars arrived at Odebolt from Canada. At that time, this marked the largest import in history of Hereford cattle into the United States, Dan Etler said.

Multiple sources, including newspapers, noted that when the cattle arrived at Brookmont Farm, the prized Herefords moved into the largest cattle barn in the United States. Likely built in 1883, the barn measured two hundred feet square and was fifty feet tall. It cost $25,000 to build (That's roughly $650,000 in today's dollars) and included stalls for seven hundred head of cattle. From the observation cupola, one could view six area towns, along with much of Sac County and Ida County, Dan Etler said.

An adjacent hay barn was competed in 1884 at Brookmont Farm. The sixteen-sided structure, similar in appearance to a railroad roundhouse, measured more than one hundred feet in diameter and thirty feet tall. The massive building was designed to hold eight hundred tons of hay. A steam-powered conveyor system transferred hay to the center of the cattle barn.

A central plant waterworks system was also completed at Brookmont Farm in 1884. A windmill pumped water from a spring at the nearby creek to a tank. Steam-powered pumps later replaced the windmills for this purpose. Water lines brought the water to the home, cattle barn and hay shed. Six-inch water mains were included to make the buildings fireproof, although this didn't prevent fires from destroying these buildings in the years ahead.

By 1885, more modern technology defined the farm, this time in the form of a telephone line that connected Brookmont Farm to Odebolt. The cattle business also gained momentum that year. The first Hereford sale by C.W. Cook & Son occurred by 1885 with J.C. Powell of Guthrie Center. By then, Brookmont Farm's Hereford herd had grown to five hundred head, the largest in the world. The Hereford "Brookmont Beauties" dominated the cattle shows at the 1885 Iowa State Fair.

BROOKMONT ENTERS A NEW ERA

Times were changing by 1891, when C.W. Cook's son, Albert Eugene Cook, began operating Brookmont Farm. This generation of the Cook family put down roots on the Odebolt-area farm.

Albert Cook became actively involved with Iowa State College's Experiment Station. Founded in 1888, the experiment station conducted research to contribute to the advancement of Iowa's agricultural industry and to improve the economic and social condition of Iowa's families and communities. Cook provided his land, livestock and facilities for research in alternative crops, livestock rations, various grains and popcorn.

In 1902, Brookmont Farm conducted its first cattle-feeding test with Iowa State. This involved 200 of the 2,000 to 2,500 cattle that were typically on the farm. The cattle were shipped to market via a special express train to Chicago, where they sold well. Newspaper headlines proclaimed, "Odebolt Is the Hub: Attention of Cattle Feeders Is Riveted on the Great Iowa Test." The feeding test was such a success that plans were made to expand these trials in the coming years. More experiments conducted in conjunction with Iowa State included a six-hundred-acre oat test and a one-hundred-acre German beer barley test in 1905.

Perhaps the barley test was inspired by a May 1903 visit to Brookmont Farm, where a German delegation sponsored by the U.S. Department of Agriculture visited the United States. The group—which included forty-three farmers, politicians and other noteworthy leaders of the day—spent two days in Iowa. The group toured the campus of Iowa State on the first day. The next day, they took a special train to Odebolt. "When delegations came to Iowa to see what farming was about and see the best, they came here," Dan Etler said.

During the German delegation's visit at Brookmont Farm, they marveled at the corncribs. In 1902, Cook had approved the construction of two massive corncribs with an innovative filling system. He was an inventor at heart, and prolific one at that. Cook worked with S.E. Kurtz, an inventor from Sac City, to create the cribs, which measured two hundred feet long and were designed to hold both ear corn (50,000 bushels) and shelled corn (100,000 bushels).

After the German guests had toured the farm, they enjoyed an authentic German meal that was served on the second floor of the farm's pavilion. The dinner (which had been planned by Cook's wife, Christina) included a new treat the Germans had never tasted before: popcorn.

Always an innovator, Albert Cook filed a patent in 1905 for the Auto-Farmer motorized disk, which he developed with S.E. Kurtz. This was among the earliest of self-propelled farm implements in the United States. It also marked the beginning of a long string of forty-three patents for Cook, Dan Etler noted.

Cook was ahead of his time in terms of viewing Brookmont as a business and organizing the farm into three divisions, including livestock, seed and crops. The central office of Brookmont Farm suggested the atmosphere of a country bank, as several clerks were busy with ledgers, blueprints and office files, according to Forrest Crissey in his article "The Business of Farming," which ran in the May 14, 1910 issue of the *Saturday Evening Post* magazine.

"The thing which spoke most loudly to me the message, 'Farming is a Business' was a set of maps, in colors, arranged in the shape of a huge calendar hanging on the wall of the private office," Crissey added. He was referring to Cook's rigorous crop/pasture planning system and crop rotation schedule. The sheer size of Brookmont Farm also impressed Crissey. "Brookmont contains 46 quarter sections," he wrote. "To drive around it would involve a journey of 14 miles."

Cook even hired two college professors to run the various divisions of Brookmont Farm, including F.R. Marshall from Kansas State to manage the cattle operation and H.M. Cottrell from Iowa State to manage the seed division. The number of farmhands boarding at Brookmont Farm varied by season, ranging from forty to one hundred men. "Perhaps Mr. Cook is prouder of nothing else than the fact that he has a Brookmont alumni of more than 100 men who came to him without funds and left him to locate on good farms of their own," Crissey added.

As time went on, Cook announced plans in 1909 to downsize Brookmont. By 1914, Cook decided to liquidate Brookmont Farm entirely and sell off all the cattle. The 188 cattle sold brought $32,629—nearly $836,000 in today's dollars. Brookmont Farm also had 1,881 acres remaining at the time of the sale at $250 per acre (roughly $6,400 per acre in today's dollars).

The Cook family's last season in Odebolt ended in 1914. The Cooks spent the rest of their lives in the Chicago area, including Evanston, Illinois. By 1918, the last remaining pieces of the farm—including the mansion, the central plant and adjacent land—were sold to J. Alva "Alvin" Reik. Thus ended Cook's Brookmont Farm after forty-five years and two generations of Cook family ownership.

Odebolt's Other Bonanza Farm: The Adams Ranch

Farming on the grand scale wasn't limited to Brookmont Farm. The Adams Ranch, south and west of town, started in 1872 when Hiram Cyrus Wheeler of Chicago bought eleven square miles of undeveloped prairie in the area now covered by Wheeler Township and Richland Township in Sac County.

Land buyers like Wheeler were a prime target when the Iowa Railroad Land Company advertised extensively in newspapers from Chicago and Cedar Rapids and beyond. A typical ad, like this one from the September 2, 1872 issue of the *Cedar Rapids Daily Republican*, read:

> *Wanted This Spring 10,000 Farmers! To improve 1.7 million acres of the very best farming lands in the world which can now be had at present value on long time with 6% interest and deferred payments. Railroad grants along the Chicago and North Western, Illinois Central and Sioux City & Pacific Railways are mainly located in the middle region of western Iowa. Noted for its salubrious climate, fever and ague being unknown, and inexhaustible soil, a finely watered yet perfectly drained district in the best agricultural state in the Union. Now is the time to secure a home at $4 or $5 per acre in the luxurious valley of either the Boyer, the Maple, the Soldier or the Little Sioux.*

Exploring tickets were available at railroad ticket offices in Chicago, Davenport, Clinton, Dubuque and Cedar Rapids, the ad noted. "County maps sent free. Send for a guide—it gives descriptions, prices, terms, locations and how to reach the lands."

Wheeler was one of the first buyers to respond. He purchased seven thousand acres in Sac County, where he planned to establish a dairy farm. The Iowa Railroad Company charged Wheeler three dollars per acre (about sixty-three dollars per acre in today's money) but gave him a discount because of the large size of his purchase, which also included one thousand acres in neighboring Crawford County and one thousand additional acres in Plymouth County in northwest Iowa, according to the self-published book *Fairview Farm History* by Kyle Hustedt.

In the early 1870s, Wheeler hired Abner Chandler as superintendent of the new Wheeler Farm (which later became known as the Adams Ranch). Chandler directed the building of the farmstead and broke sod so wheat and oats could be planted. Hiring farm managers like Chandler distinguished America's bonanza farms from smaller farms. "An outstanding feature of the bonanza farm was the large degree to which it used professional management," noted Hiram M. Drache, author of the book *The Day of the Bonanza*.

In its early years, the Wheeler Ranch produced flax, prompting the establishment of the J.B. Winslow and Son flax mill in Odebolt in 1880. The ranch also became a pioneer in popcorn production and included fine

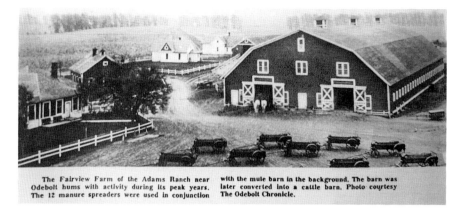

The Fairview Farm of the Adams Ranch near Odebolt hums with activity during its peak years. The 12 manure spreaders were used in conjunction with the mule barn in the background. The barn was later converted into a cattle barn. Photo courtesy The Odebolt Chronicle.

The numerous manure spreaders on the Adams Ranch near Odebolt were used in conjunction with the mule barn shown here. *Author's collection.*

livestock, including Percheron horses, English Shire stallions, Clydesdale horses and colts and Shorthorn cattle.

Wheeler ran for governor of Iowa on the Republican ticket in 1891 but lost to Horace Boies, a Democrat. Following this setback, Wheeler's star was on the wane. By 1896, Wheeler had sold the farm to William P. Adams, who paid $200,000 (about $6.1 million today) for ten sections of land he named Fairview Farm.

Adams was familiar with bonanza farming, thanks to his father, John, who owned a 9,600-acre operation known as Fairview Farm in southeast North Dakota that produced wheat and sheep. By 1899, the financial account for Adams's Sac County farm—which produced corn, wheat and livestock—showed a profit of more than $50,855 (more than $1.5 million in today's money).

Like Brookmont Farm, Fairview Farm (which was commonly known as the Adams Ranch) was a showplace. Hundreds of beautiful shade trees lined the roadways and fences. Thousands of sheep (50,000 to 100,000 sheep, depending on various historical accounts) were a big part of Fairview Farm in the early 1900s. The long rows of sheep barns were painted with the words "Feed My Lambs." It wasn't uncommon for neighbors to take a Sunday drive for a sightseeing trip along the roads that passed by Fairview Farm.

"An impressive farm in every way, the beauty of the entire 10 sections is wonderfully divided by the elm trees which line both sides of every road for a total of 54 miles," noted an article called "The Beef Factory" that appeared in the 1954 *American Hereford Journal.*

By 1913, W.P. Adams had expanded his Iowa farm to twelve sections of land. The farm employed between 45 men in the winter months to 150 men in the busiest months. Farming with mules was another distinctive feature of Fairview Farm that would last for decades. By the early 1900s, the farm included 120 teams of mules to pull equipment and assist with other farm work.

Bonanza farms like the Adams Ranch could also afford the most modern machinery and were early adopters of the latest ag technology to help the business become even more efficient. In 1925, Adams introduced fifteen one-row corn pickers pulled by steel-wheeled tractors. "This improved corn harvesting over the use of 76 wagons pulled by 27 teams of mules four abreast, with men walking and husking corn for 60 days, averaging 60 bushels per day per man," noted Sandra Kessler Host, author of the book *Adams Ranch Story: 1872–1964.*

In addition to running his farm, W.P. Adams built a bank in Odebolt and served as the bank's president. He became an avid traveler in his later years, spending the winters in Miami, Florida, and cruising the world on ocean liners. He died in Miami Beach in 1937 at age seventy-four.

When W.P.'s son, Bob, took over the Adams Ranch, he and his wife raised their three children on the farm. Bob Adams indulged himself with fine saddle horses and built a barn and a training track for the horses. He also became a director of the American Horse Breeders Association. From time to time, he traveled to Missouri to buy mules for the farm, including one time after a 1945 fire destroyed the Adams Ranch's mule barn and killed many mules.

Due to labor shortages on the farm during World War II, one hundred prisoners of war were sent to the farm to help in the fields. One of the biggest changes at Adams Ranch, however, was the herd of commercial cattle that arrived in the 1940s. "Visualizing the full potential of this productive, Corn Belt farm, Adams in 1946 decided that beef cattle should be added to the program of grain production," noted the 1954 *American Hereford Journal.* "A trip to the Omaha market resulted in the purchase of the first Herefords on the farm. This new venture went hand and hand with the program long in effect of building the soil to higher productivity each year."

This program included all sections of the farm and involved a five-year rotation. "It begins with a section planted to oats with a seeding of legumes and grasses, the oats, of course, being harvested," the article stated. "The second year finds that section furnishing plenty of hay, which is cut and baled. The third year this 640-acre tract is pastured by cows and calves. The fourth and fifth years are given over entirely to the growing of corn, the grasses having been plowed under at the beginning of the fourth year. The plowing under of the lush pastures provides the soil with a conditioning that results in higher yields of corn, grain and grasses in their regular turns."

The article praised the efficiency of the Adams Ranch, thanks to its owner and two farm superintendents, Page Rector and Luther Miller, who oversaw a crew of thirty-two farmhands. "Absolutely everything moves with the precision and smoothness that is essential in the operation of this complete Beef Factory," noted the article.

After Bob Adams died of a heart attack in 1956, the Adams Ranch was left to his oldest son, William Phipps "Bill" Adams II, in a trust. Bill would be the last generation of his family to own the Adams Ranch. He was passionate about Hereford cattle and decided to sell the Iowa farm so he could purchase six thousand acres of land near Valentine, Nebraska, to graze cattle.

In 1964, Charles Lakin of Emerson, Iowa, bought the entire Adams Ranch (6,510 acres) for $2.5 million—close to $400 per acre. (That's roughly $3,300 per acre in today's dollars.) Lakin, who had a reputation more as a land developer than a farmer, soon began selling off parcels of the Adams Ranch. By 1975, Lakin had conveyed the warranty deed of the original Adams Ranch property to Shinrone Incorporated of Detroit, Michigan, for $4 million. They invested another $250,000 and expanded the ranch's cattle feeding operation. By the 1980s, however, the original Adams Ranch was sold off in parcels to various farmers and other landowners.

By the time Bill Adams died in 1996, an article in the *Des Moines Register* titled "Last Owner of Iowa's Adams' Ranch Dies" noted that "the farm was broken up during the recession of the 1980s and sold as several smaller farms."

While there are few traces of the Adams Ranch left standing on the landscape, Sac County's bonanza farms were the forerunners of today's modern agribusiness, said Host, a retired teacher and social worker who lives in Council Bluffs. "Rural Iowa has so many fantastic, untold stories like this. It's important to teach this local history."

Chapter 6

RURAL IOWA ENTERS THE TWENTIETH CENTURY

J
ust as Sac County's bonanza farms embraced a scientific, business-focused approach to farming by the late 1800s, more farmers across Iowa had also adopted this mind-set by the early twentieth century. This was due, in part, to an innovative system of "corn gospel trains" that would become a forerunner of today's university extension service.

In 1903, corn maturation in Iowa was slowed by a cool, wet growing season followed by an early frost. Farmers and seed dealers were concerned about the viability of seed for the 1904 growing season. Perry Holden, who had joined Iowa State College's faculty in 1902 as the professor of agronomy and vice dean of agriculture, organized a huge seed testing project in Ames, where seed samples were submitted by growers. Results showed that more than half of the seed was not viable.

In April 1904, Holden shared these shocking results with attendees at an Iowa seed dealers' conference in Des Moines. Holden proposed to go to farmers across Iowa via special trains provided by the railroads so he could share advice on how to select, test and plant corn for the best chance of success that year.

On April 18, 1904, the first "corn gospel train" left Des Moines with Holden and his assistants on board. They headed to northwest Iowa, where crop conditions were the worst. The train included the locomotive, a private lodging car, an "instruction car" that could hold one hundred people, and a car for media and railroad officials.

Iowa State College professor Perry Holden addressed Iowa farmers during a crop production lecture in a train car on March 5, 1909, at Emmetsburg. *Courtesy of Palo Alto County Historical Museum.*

The train's first stop on this three-day trip was in Gowrie, where more than two hundred farmers were waiting. Half of the crowd stood outside in the snow by the open windows on the train to hear Holden's important information, which featured the message "Test, don't guess."

Each stop lasted twenty to thirty minutes. Then the train quickly departed for the next stop. In the first three days, Holden and his team gave sixty presentations. Additional educational seminars (and instructors) were added on future corn gospel train excursions to meet the demand for this valuable information.

On March 13, 1905, a corn gospel train that started in Sioux City made twelve stops along its southeasterly route, including Lake City, its final stop of the day. A March 16, 1905 edition of the *Lake City Graphic* included the front-page article "Corn Gospel at Lake City: 500 Farmers in Attendance." "The meeting was a greater success than had been anticipated," the article noted. "The audience was captivated. Prof. Holden, when asked how much more corn he thought Iowa could be made to produce, based his estimate upon the supposition that the average amount of corn produced by each acre in Iowa could be increased from 33 bushels to 50 bushels."

The article also noted farmers' changing attitudes toward farm management. "Prof. Holden thinks the idea of scientific farming will have to work itself into popularity. If one farmer in a community tests his seed corn this year, his neighbors will naturally watch the results of the test. If his crop is better than the average, or even if he has secured a better stand because of his efforts in the selections of seed, his neighbors will try it next year, and thus the gospel will grow until all of the farmers will have been converted to it."

The article added that this spirit of improvement would affect all crop production in Iowa, not just corn. "Joe Trigg, one of the leading advocates of higher agriculture in Iowa who is traveling with Prof. Holden, said that the movement now in progress of spreading the seed corn gospel was the greatest in its direction that had ever been undertaken in any state. He said it would grow on all sides until it reached around the world and would add millions to the annual product of the soil. He said it would grow to be of more importance as the country became more thickly settled and the land grew more valuable, because more would be required from each acre. He declared the question of the future every man engaged in the tilling of the soil will be: 'How much can I add to the world's food supply?'"

The Birth of Extension

By May 1905, Holden and his staff had delivered 1,235 talks to nearly 150,000 farmers across Iowa. They had covered the entire state by the end of 1906. The success of this effort was widely acclaimed and marked the first extension service outreach in America, bringing knowledge from the college to the people of the state.

In 1906, the Iowa legislature enacted the Agricultural Extension Act, making funds available for scientific demonstration projects. It is believed this was the first specific legislation establishing state extension work, according to Iowa State University (ISU).

By 1912, the need for full-time extension agents was becoming apparent. The legislature enacted the Farm Aid Association Act in 1913. The law permitted, and later required, each county to appropriate funds for county extension work. The bill required each county to have a local sponsor, and the county Farm Bureau filled that role.

When the U.S. Congress passed the Smith-Lever Act in 1914, Iowa was ready to accept the provisions and benefits of the new law. The Smith-Lever Act established a national Cooperative Extension Service that extended outreach programs through land-grant universities to educate rural Americans about advances in agricultural practices and technology. These advances helped increase American agricultural productivity dramatically throughout the twentieth century.

By 1918, each Iowa county had a county extension worker in place. Staff positions were soon developed to provide leadership for home economics and 4-H program efforts.

INVISIBLE ASSETS: THE UNTOLD STORY OF IOWA'S AG DRAINAGE SYSTEMS

While Iowa farmers were learning that scientific farming was vital to boosting corn yields, they knew proper drainage of the soil was equally important, if not more so.

Drainage was an especially big issue in of parts of northern and west-central Iowa, the so-called prairie pothole region, where glaciers' actions thousands of years ago had created an extensive network of wetlands. While these wetlands play a role in the ecology of the region, they also created big challenges for Iowa's settlers and, later, the farmers.

When Iowa's earliest roads became rutted and impassable, or if a person were heading into an area where no roads existed at all, the traveler might strike off across the prairie. Frequently, these travelers' paths would cross a prairie wetland. Here they would be stopped by the soft ground and stagnant water (or ice, depending on the weather). Wagons and livestock would stay trapped in the mire, waiting a helping hand or drier weather to get out of the muck.

The wetlands were also breeding grounds for mosquitos that could carry disease. An exhibit at the State Historical Museum of Iowa in Des Moines tells the story of Mary Ann Davidson, who settled on the frontier of Marshall County in central Iowa in 1846: "[T]he hum and stings of millions of musquetoes [sic] and the shrill notes of the whippowils [sic] bore us company through the night," she noted.

Many of Iowa's settlers promoted the advantages of draining excess water from the state's land. Underground drainage was encouraged as a means to improve the health of livestock and farm families by "preventing injuries to cattle and other stock, corresponding to the effects produced upon human beings by the marsh miasma, chills, and colds, thus inducing a general low state of health, and—in extreme cases—the rot," according to the Fourth Annual Report of the Iowa State Agricultural Society in 1857.

Ag drainage started transforming the Iowa landscape by the late 1800s. If there were a *Mysteries at the Museum* television series geared toward agriculture, a certain item on display at the Greene County Historical Society's museum in Jefferson would be ideal to lead in a segment. It's hollow, it's made of clay, it contains a message from the past and it was buried in the ground for decades. It's a unique clay drainage tile dated to 1885. The message carved around the exterior of the tile reads, "We the men who started the tile work did so with a motive to benefit the town and country. Signed T.P. LaRue of Scranton, Iowa."

An interpretive sign by the tile shares a quote from S.J. Melson, a former Greene County engineer, to explain the curious item's history: "This tile was placed into my hands by Carl Paup on February 1968. Mr. Paup stated the tile was unearthed and has lasted for many years on the property owned and operated by Harrison Paup of Kendrick Township, Greene County, Iowa."

An exhibit at the Greene County Historical Society in Jefferson shows the importance of tile drainage to Iowa agriculture. This unique clay drainage tile, dated 1885, came from a field near Scranton. *Author's collection.*

That tile reflects a major part of Iowa's agricultural history that has been buried, literally, for generations, yet this history continues to influence farming methods, especially in the prairie pothole regions of north-central Iowa and northwest Iowa. "In general, ag drainage in Iowa got its start around 1880, but this varied a lot, depending on the region," said Joe Otto, a historian and PhD candidate at the University of Oklahoma who works as a communications specialist with the Iowa Water Center at Iowa State University.

The first documented case of a drain tile being installed in Iowa occurred in 1868 on the grounds of Iowa State College in Ames, Otto added. Before that, some of the first drainage ditches were dug in the 1850s along the Mississippi River in Des Moines County, just upstream from Burlington, so farmers could help protect themselves from flooding. One of these farmers, John Williams, was later elected to the state legislature and helped get the state's first drainage laws passed in the 1870s, Otto said.

DRAINAGE AFFECTED IOWA'S SETTLEMENT PATTERNS

Ag drainage was such a major issue in the 1800s that it affected Iowa's settlement. "Iowa wasn't settled east to west, but from the bottoms up to the top of the state's many river valleys," Otto said. "Atop the river valleys were the flat, glaciated prairies of north-central and northwestern Iowa. These were settled and farmed starting in the 1870s and 1880s—several decades after farming started along the Mississippi River."

The region's extensive swamps and sloughs were remnants of the last glacier, which loosened its icy grip on Iowa about twelve thousand years ago. "There was a lot of water and nowhere for it to go," Otto said. "Drainage ditches had to be dug and tile lines had to be laid before the sloughs and swamps of Iowa could be farmed. This started around 1880 and picked up speed in the early 1900s as drainage technology became more advanced."

Ag leaders like Civil War veteran and pioneer farmer Jesse Allee, who settled in the Newell area in 1871, knew that ag drainage would be essential to the development and prosperity of the region. "He was far-seeing with the unshakable belief in the future of the community's farm land," noted the 1969 Newell centennial history book at the Allee Mansion south of Newell. "Jesse worked hard educating the public to the necessity of proper drainage if this area was to be a leader in agriculture."

Settlers in Greene County faced a similar situation. "By 1880, many landowners realized underground drainage tile was needed to remove the excess water," wrote James H. Andrew, a longtime Greene County farmer who created a farm drainage tiling exhibit at the Greene County Historical Society's museum in Jefferson before he passed away in 2014.

As more settlers moved into Iowa and demand for tile drainage grew, tile kilns and factories popped up across the state, Otto noted. Greene County, like many Iowa counties, had multiple firms manufacturing clay tile. These businesses used locally sourced clay to produce drainage tiles, bricks and more.

Ag drainage in Iowa took a major leap forward in 1904, when state legislation provided for the formation of drainage districts. "Farmers could always drain their own lands if they wanted to, but to truly manage drained water meant cooperation with your neighbors," Otto said.

A group of farmers could petition for a drainage district. An engineer would survey the land to establish the boundaries of the area, and a feasible drainage plan would be developed. If approved, a contract would be drawn up, with the cost paid by assessing each landowner for his or her fair share, considering his needs and the acres involved. The county acted as the administrator of the drainage district and assessed taxes against the land, as needed, to pay for the initial cost and later for the maintenance of the drainage district. Many times, the money would be borrowed by issuing bonds, and the landowners would make payments on a ten-year plan, Andrew noted.

The 1910s became the golden age of ag drainage when most of Iowa's public drainage systems were built, Otto added. "By 1912, Iowa's farmers had spent more money on drainage than the U.S. government spent to build the Panama Canal."

Around 1923, the first tiling machines started to be used, although hand digging of tile lines continued for many years, Andrew noted. In the spring, summer and fall, men could find a job "in the ditch" if they wanted to work. "Many immigrants coming to the USA found their first jobs digging canals, and later drainage ditches. You didn't have to know English to be a good man in the ditch," added Andrew, who noted that many of these workers were from Sweden and Ireland.

As ag drainage issues have increasingly become intertwined with debates about conservation and water quality, it's important to keep the line of communication open between farmers and urban residents, Otto said. "I think the harsh reaction against ag drainage that's happened in the past few years is due in part to people suddenly wanting to engage in drainage matters, but unsure of what drainage is and does, who administers it and what powers they have. On the other side of the coin, the people trusted to manage the public's interests in drainage have a responsibility to break down barriers, explain misconceptions and guide the conversation to a common ground."

That's a big reason why Andrew documented the history of ag tiling, counting it as one of the most important events in local history and the settlement of the region, noted his son, Jim Andrew of Jefferson. "Think of the men and the effort it took to dig the clay, form and cure the tile, haul the tile to the jobsite, the survey crews working in ponds and swamps, the drainage plans made by the drainage engineer proving drainage was practical, the legal problems of objections and disputes, letting the bids, and, most important, the hundreds of men with strong backs who worked digging the ditches, laying the tile and filling the ditches," wrote James H. Andrew.

"Yet, the tile is hidden underground, and the 'Iron Men' tilers are all deceased," he concluded. "As time passes, there is little appreciation for the cooperative efforts that drained Greene County and made it so productive. Only when these old tile systems fail and have to be replaced at great expense will many people realize the generous gifts we've received from the drainage district system."

THE GOLDEN ERA OF AGRICULTURE

Ag drainage from the late 1800s into the early 1900s coincided with the so-called Golden Age of Agriculture, the period between 1897 and 1918 when Iowa agriculture moved from a primitive means of survival to a modern business venture.

As the American urban population expanded in the early years of the century, the need for farm products increased. With growing numbers of urban workers, money was available to purchase farm products to feed the ever-growing urban population. During this period, Iowa farmers attained high levels of production and received good prices for their products.

In 1910, the average increase in prices received for all kinds of farm produce was 87 percent higher than in 1900, while the cost of equipment and basic necessities had increased only 5 percent, according to the Explorations in Iowa History Project from the University of Northern

Iowa. In 1916, more than half (53 percent) of the livestock received at markets in Chicago came from Iowa.

Iowa also led the nation in corn and oat production. With money to spend, Iowa farm families purchased equipment for both the farm business and the farm home. Farm families could afford to live with a certain degree of personal comfort. Many rural families purchased their first automobile during this time.

In 1908, Stallie DeLong of Yetter, Iowa, paid $1,250 (the equivalent of nearly $35,000 today) for a two-cylinder Jackson automobile. This was such a momentous occasion that he and his wife, Nettie, took their children out of school for the day so a photographer from Rockwell City could take a photo of the family with their new car in front of their farmhouse northeast of Yetter. (Due to the poor roads that covered most of Iowa at the time, however, the car was stored on blocks much of the year.)

Poor roads that contributed to isolation in rural America were a sign that all was not well in farm country, however, even during the golden age. President Theodore Roosevelt believed rural America was the "backbone of our nation's efficiency," but he was concerned that rural life risked being left behind in the modern America emerging in the first decade of the twentieth century.

Yetter-area farmer Stallie DeLong paid $1,250 in 1908 for this two-cylinder Jackson automobile, the first car in Elm Grove Township, Calhoun County. *Courtesy of Harold DeLong.*

In 1908, Roosevelt formed a Commission on Country Life, headed up by Liberty Hyde Bailey, dean of the New York State College of Agriculture at Cornell, to investigate ways of making country life more attractive. Bailey described the country life movement as "the working out of the desire to make rural civilization as effective and satisfying as other civilization." Roosevelt also asked well-known ag journalist "Uncle Henry" Wallace of Des Moines to serve with the Country Life Commission. Wallace, who was in his early seventies and still actively involved with *Wallaces' Farmer* magazine, agreed.

The commission held thirty public hearings throughout the country, circulated more than 500,000 brief questionnaires and held numerous other meetings to get a clearer picture of life in rural America, noted Cornell University. The 1909 *Report of the Country Life Commission* highlighted a list of deficiencies in rural life that were prompting people to leave the country for the city. The commission offered three recommendations: a nationalized extension service, which was formalized by the passage of the Smith-Lever Act in 1914; continuing fact-finding surveys, fostering the development of agricultural economics and rural sociology in universities and the federal government; and a campaign for rural progress.

Not only was the report influential and widely quoted in its time, but its legacy has not been forgotten. "The Report of the Country Life Commission remains a landmark for the attention it brought to issues of country life," noted Stanford University's Rural West Initiative.

RURAL FREE DELIVERY CONNECTS FARMERS TO THE WORLD

One advantage rural families enjoyed by the time the Country Life Commission formed was free rural mail delivery. This type of service was unheard of until the 1890s.

By 1890, nearly 41 million people (65 percent of the American population) lived in rural areas, according to the United States Postal Service (USPS). Although many city dwellers had enjoyed free home delivery since 1863, rural citizens had to pick up their mail at the post office in town.

Before the advent of radio, television, mobile phones and e-mail, rural America was a terribly isolated place. In some places, farms were miles apart, and poor roads made traveling to town an all-day chore. That's one of the reasons why trips into town to pick up or send mail were rarely made more than once a week.

By 1896, the U.S. Congress had appropriated enough money for the post office to bring rural free delivery (RFD). By 1899, Iowa had established twenty-three routes, according to the Iowa Pathways project of Iowa PBS.

RFD brought the world to the Iowa countryside. Farmers could get news, market updates and more via letters, newspapers and magazines like *Successful Farming*, which Edwin Thomas (E.T.) Meredith founded in Des Moines in 1902.

Farm families also looked forward to mail-order catalogues from national retailers including Sears, Roebuck and Company and Montgomery Ward. RFD and the Sears catalogue, in particular, were a perfect match. The first Sears, Roebuck and Co. catalogue was printed in 1893. Within the next three years, the company began printing spring and fall catalogues filled with farm equipment, sewing machines, hand-cranked washing machines, musical instruments, saddles, firearms, buggies, bicycles, baby carriages, books, clothing, watches, jewelry, sporting goods, groceries and more.

In 1905, the "Iowazation" plan began. Company founder Richard W. Sears excelled at innovative marketing strategies. Sears asked his best

Rural free delivery helped alleviate some of the isolation of rural Iowa. Rural mail carrier John McCreary, who served the Lake City area, is shown circa 1914. *Courtesy of Judy Hungate.*

customers in Iowa to distribute twenty-four catalogues among their friends and neighbors. In return, they earned a small percentage of the resulting sales. The "Iowazation" program proved so successful that it was used in other states, as well.

Within a few years, the Sears catalogue had become so popular that local merchants in small towns across Iowa and the nation lost a great deal of business to mail-order companies. Volume sales kept merchandise prices low, and a reassuring money-back guarantee won over customers. Iowa's small-town business owners launched "trade at home" campaigns to compete with Sears and Montgomery Ward. They purchased ads in local newspapers encouraging shoppers to buy from their local stores.

The Gordon–Van Tine Company of Davenport, Iowa, supplied the precut pieces for this barn on the Ed Binkert farm. The barn was shipped to Lake City via the railroad. After local carpenters completed the barn on August 16, 1928, the family hosted a barn dance there. *Courtesy of Rod Laidler.*

While RFD fueled an "Amazon effect" that disrupted retail business of the era, it also created a unique opportunity for farmers: the chance to buy a new barn by mail. In the days before home power tools, precut buildings represented an enormous saving in labor and materials for the builder. Manufacturers claimed that the precut system would save the builder up to 30 percent compared to the cost of standard building methods.

By the early 1900s, companies like Montgomery Ward; Sears, Roebuck and Company; and Gordon–Van Tine of Davenport, Iowa, as well as others, were supplying mail-order barns and other farm buildings. Included in the Gordon–Van Tine 1909 catalogue were two round barns, three gambrel-roof barns, one cross-gable barn, poultry houses, a granary, an icehouse, a corncrib, a hog house and an implement shed.

The company's 1918 catalogue, *Photographs and Letters: Some Gordon–Van Tine Barns and What Their Owners Think of Them,* included testimonials from various farmers, including John Schneider of Wheatland, Iowa. Schneider owned No. 224, a sixty-foot-by-eighty-four-foot, gambrel-roof barn that cost $2,400 (more than $48,000 in today's dollars). "Gentleman, we have finished putting up our barn," Schneider wrote the Gordon–Van Tine Company on May 31, 1918. "We are well satisfied with the lumber and material we bought of you. Everyone who has seen the barn says that it is a dandy."

At its peak, Gordon–Van Tine employed 350 people. By 1946, the once-thriving company had been sold to a Cincinnati salvage company that liquidated the firm.

Today, discovering and authenticating mail-order barns isn't easy. The Prairie Pedlar north of Odebolt features a Sears mail-order barn. "One of the students who attended Cook #8 country school recalled that construction on this barn started in 1941," said Jane Hogue, who runs the Prairie Pedlar garden with her husband, Jack. "The year 1943 is carved into the cement threshold by the barn door. Perhaps the final touches were completed that year."

Chapter 7

THE CULTURE OF IOWA AGRICULTURE

Just as mail-order barns have become a rarity, so have other elements that once defined rural life in Iowa, including country schools.

Historically, Iowa has been a state that values education. Perhaps nowhere was this more visible than in the network of country schools that developed in every county in Iowa in the 1800s. With an astonishing twelve to fourteen thousand country schools at one time, depending on what report you use, Iowa had more one-room schoolhouses than any other state in the union, according to the Iowa Department of Education. Each country school's district covered a four-mile-square area, and children attended the local school in their area. This way, no child would be more than two miles away from any school.

Teaching school was one of the few occupations single women were allowed to enter. In the heyday of the country schools, teachers needed little more than a basic education themselves.

Rural children did not legally have to attend school until 1902, and many didn't. In many farm families, parents perceived education as a luxury, while work was a necessity. They may also have believed that farm work was an education in and of itself, preparing their children for a lifetime of labor. In 1889, more than a decade before Iowa passed a compulsory education law, 75 percent of Iowa's school-age children were enrolled in school, but only 47 percent attended, noted Pamela Riney-Kehrberg, a history professor at Iowa State University.

Older farm boys often stayed home to help with the crops and only went to school in the winter. May Lacey grew up on a Palo Alto County farm in northwest Iowa, and her brothers were a part of that half of all Iowa children who did not attend school. "The children had their work to do as soon as it was possible for them to work," wrote Lacey, whose memories were recorded in the 1948 article "Pioneer Life in Palo Alto County" in the *Iowa Journal of History and Politics*. "Brother Fred took a man's place from the time he was 10 years old, and Frank followed suit, though he did have a little better chance for schooling since he attended a few spring terms."

The records of the North Liberty School in Iowa Township in Cedar County show a pattern of attendance that was typical of many country schools, Riney-Kehrberg said. In the spring of 1877, thirty-nine children attended the school. Of those, twelve were boys, and only three of those boys were over the age of nine. None of the three teenage boys attended more than fourteen days out of a three-month term.

In some cases, farm girls missed a fair amount of school, especially on Mondays, when they were needed at home to help with the labor-intensive chore of laundry. (Weekly chores in many homes followed a regimented schedule of wash on Monday, iron on Tuesday, mend on Wednesday, churn butter on Thursday, clean on Friday, bake on Saturday, rest on Sunday.)

Even in families that valued education, achieving that education could be difficult. Rosa Armentrout, whose family lived in eastern Iowa near Wilton, despaired at times of completing her education. She loved school, writing often in her diary about her fellow students and their daily activities. In 1877, shortly before she turned sixteen, she wrote, "I am going to school now. We have splendid times at school. We play charades and ball and everything else almost every day. I study reading, grammar, geography, physiology, arithmetic and writing."

Her love of education, however, could not always overcome the barriers between her and the schoolhouse door, noted Riney-Kehrberg in her article "Helping Ma and Helping Pa: Iowa's Turn-of-the-Century Farm Children," which appeared in spring 2000 issue of *The Annals of Iowa*.

Sometimes Mother Nature was the culprit. Wet weather often rendered dirt roads and farm fields impossibly—and impassibly—muddy. After a night of torrential rain, "the sloughs were so bad that Mother wouldn't let me go," wrote Armentrout. When the rain continued the next day, her despair was clear. "No one knows how bad I wanted to go to school today. The men were actually too lazy to put the bed on the wagon so they could take me."

Then there was the serious matter of illness. When her mother became ill in the summer of 1877, Armentrout's opportunity for education was curtailed again, since she was needed at home. Fortunately, Armentrout's mother recovered. Armentrout herself was eventually able to complete her schooling and grew up to be Dr. Rosa Armentrout Butterfield.

Given the high disease rates of the late nineteenth and early twentieth centuries, it's not surprising that many children lost days, weeks and even months of school to illness, Riney-Kehrberg noted. In 1880, Ella F. Campbell of Lucas County wrote, "My sister Susie died this winter of diphtheria and lung fever, and I had it very bad at the same time, so that I could not go to the funeral. I am going to school now. I did not go this winter on account of my sickness."

COUNTRY SCHOOL DAYS FROM A FARM BOY'S PERSPECTIVE

As technology advanced in the twentieth century, complete with labor-saving devices like self-propelled tractors, cars, improved roads and medical advances, it became easier for rural children to attend school on a much more regular basis.

From 1939 to 1947, James Graham attended Penn No. 3, a one-room country schoolhouse in northwestern Madison County, south of Dexter. As a student at Penn No. 3, Graham followed in the footsteps of his forebearers. His father, James C. Graham, attended from 1906 to 1914, while Graham's grandfather George Graham was a student there in the 1870s, around the time George's sister, Lillie, taught at the school.

James Graham walked a mile to school on a hilly, often-muddy country road. "There were approximately 12 kids from the little six-year-old first graders to the 14-year-old eight graders who attended our country school," Graham wrote in his self-published book, *Dexter, Iowa: Stories and Memories*.

Even though the students got along well, one time Graham put a cocklebur in a girl's hair. "Our teacher came down really hard on me," he wrote. "I spent several recesses writing, 'I will not tease the girls,' on the blackboard while the other kids were outside having fun. I never teased the girls again."

Like many Iowa country schools, Penn No. 3 had rows of wooden desks, with the younger kids in the front and older students in the back rows. The teacher's large wooden desk stood in front of the slate blackboard. Portraits of George Washington and Abraham Lincoln hung on the wall, along with a large, wind-up clock. The school also housed an upright piano and a wind-up phonograph.

"Almost all my school time at Penn #3 was without electricity," Graham said. "We thought nothing about it." Three large windows on the east side of the school and another three on the south provided plenty of light for reading and other schoolwork, even on the darkest winter days.

Class would start after the teacher rang her small bell. After all the students went to their seats, they would stand to recite the Pledge of Allegiance. Then it was time for music. "We all sang the song on the phonograph, but as it wound down, the song would go slower and s-l-o-w-e-r," Graham said. "The teacher would rush over and quickly wind it up again."

After music, the teacher would start with the first-grade lessons and proceed with each class through eighth grade. Each class would be called to the front of the classroom, where the teacher would work with the students on their lessons. Meanwhile, the other students worked independently on their own lessons at their desks. They used Big Chief notebooks filled with blue-lined paper pages. "These we could buy almost anywhere, even in Dexter, for five cents each," Graham recalled.

Penn No. 3 students got two recess periods each school day: one fifteen-minute session in the morning and another in the afternoon. The children went outside to play, no matter the season. Popular games included "fox and geese" (a game of tag) and Annie-Annie Over, where a ball was thrown over the schoolhouse.

Back inside the school, a large coal-burning stove stood in the front of the classroom. "In extremely cold weather, the teacher would have all of us sit around the stove until it warmed up the classroom," Graham said.

Not only did Penn No. 3 have no electricity, but it had no running water. Students were assigned to fetch water from the Bloomquist farm not far from the school. The restrooms were outhouses behind the school. The one on the left was for boys, while the one on the right was for girls. "They stunk during warm weather and were very cold in the winter," Graham said. "When you went to the toilet, you didn't stay very long."

While Penn No. 3 had few amenities, it did have a party-line telephone. "It was on a mutual farm line with eight other subscribers," recalled Graham, who noted that subscribers had their own rings, with Penn No. 3 being three short rings. "If you wanted to call another line, you would have to ring one long ring to alert the operator at Dexter. You would then tell the operator who you wanted, and she would ring it for you. Crude, but it worked very well."

Students brought their own lunch to school, mostly sandwiches made with leftovers from supper the night before. In the winter, Penn No. 3 had a "hot

Hickory Grove - 1917

These photos show the Hickory Grove country school in Wright County in 1917. By the early 1900s, there were more than twelve thousand country schools like this across Iowa. *Courtesy of Heartland Museum.*

lunch program" of sorts. Students were encouraged to bring soup or other food that could be warmed up in a canning jar. "The school had a small, kerosene stove in which the teacher would put a pan of water to heat with all our jars of food," Graham said. "By noon, all was hot and very tasty. Sometimes a jar would get too hot and break, and some kid would miss their hot lunch."

To be eligible for high school, country school students had to pass an eighth-grade exam. (Students who attended school in town didn't have to take a similar exam to advance to high school.) Madison County country school students who passed their exams were invited to Winterset, the county seat, to receive their eighth-grade diplomas. "This was a very big honor," Graham recalled.

School consolidations, which marked the beginning of the end for Iowa's country schools, started occurring shortly after the turn of the twentieth century. For example, the Lytton community in west-central Iowa voted for a consolidated school district comprising forty-four sections of land. A $150,000 bond issue was approved, and students began attending classes in the new consolidated school building in Lytton in the winter of 1921–22.

The curriculum was brought to twelve grades, with a full course of study, including Latin.

The last one-room schoolhouses closed their doors permanently in 1967 through legislative decree (although some one-room schoolhouses are still operating in Iowa today, functioning as private schools operated by Amish and Mennonite groups). The legacy of Iowa's country schools lives on, however, in the thousands of lives they touched and the value of education (including higher education) they instilled in generations of rural Iowans.

Country Churches Kept the Faith

Just as country schools were interwoven into the fabric of rural Iowa for generations, so were country churches. Iowa's settlers and immigrants brought their Christian faith with them to the prairies of Iowa, as reflected in the various denominations of country churches, including Lutheran, Methodist, Presbyterian, Catholic and others.

While many rural churches have closed due to the declining population in rural Iowa, some endure. Perhaps the most famous is the Little Brown Church in the Vale near Nashua in northeast Iowa.

The church's roots date back to 1848. After World War I, as more people had cars and roads were improved, the Little Brown Church in the Vale became a popular tourist attraction and wedding venue. When a school superintendent and a merchant's daughter were married at the church years ago, a new tradition was started: the ringing of the church bell. In August 2014, the 74,000th wedding was held at the historic church site.

Another country church of note sits in the midst of Iowa's largest metropolitan area, yet its connection to rural Iowa makes sense when you know that the Church of the Land is at Living History Farms in Urbandale. It was the site of Pope John Paul II's historic visit to Iowa in 1979, and it all went back to a Truro, Iowa farmer named Joe Hays.

In 1979, Hays sat at his kitchen table to write Pope John Paul II a letter. He knew that the pontiff's American pilgrimage would occur that year. He thought a trip to America's heartland made sense. But what chance did a farmer have, inviting the pope to rural Iowa?

Perhaps a once-in-a-lifetime chance, it turned out. When Pope John Paul II left America's East Coast cities to come to Des Moines, nearly 350,000 people gathered in the fields surrounding Living History Farms on October 4, 1979,

Pope John Paul II visited Living History Farms in Urbandale on October 4, 1979. A letter from Joseph Hays, a farmer from Truro, Iowa, persuaded Pope John Paul II to come to Iowa. *Courtesy of Living History Farms.*

to hear the spiritual leader. A chill wind blew as the pope celebrated a harvest-time Mass and detailed the reasons why the church highly esteems farmers. The sacred event inspired reverence in Catholics and non-Catholics alike.

"I was a college student at Iowa State University at the time and was one of the thousands of non-Catholics who attended the Mass," said Bill Northey, a farmer from Spirit Lake, former Iowa secretary of agriculture and current U.S. Department of Agriculture undersecretary of farm production and conservation. "The Pope's visit was a very important event for Iowa."

During his visit to Iowa, the pope praised farmers' role in feeding a hungry world. "You who are farmers are stewards of a gift from God, which was intended for the good of all humanity. You have the potential to provide food for the millions who have nothing to eat, and thus help to rid the world of famine."

ORPHAN TRAIN HERITAGE INFLUENCED RURAL IOWA

Christian values and connections to the world beyond rural Iowa came together in another part of Iowa's history through the orphan trains. For more than seventy-five years, thousands of Iowa families in small towns and farms played crucial roles in the forerunner of the modern foster care system, thanks to the orphan trains.

From 1854 to 1929, a network of orphan trains relocated nearly 250,000 children from East Coast orphanages in cities like Boston and New York City to the forty-eight continental states, according to the National Orphan Train Complex in Concordia, Kansas. "The best of all asylums for the outcast child is the farmer's home," said Charles Loring Brace, a Protestant minister who founded the Children's Aid Society in New York City and developed the orphan-train concept in the 1850s.

About eight to ten thousand of these needy children were brought to Iowa to live with both farmers and town residents, according to Madonna Harms, former archivist of the Iowa Orphan Train Research Center and Archives.

When I interviewed Harms at her home in Rolfe in 2002, she told me that orphan children were taken in by families in at least 316 Iowa towns, including Adel, Algona, Ames, Barnum, Boone, Coon Rapids, Dakota City, Dougherty, Eagle Grove, Fort Dodge, Emmetsburg, Garner, Harlan, Iowa Falls, Manson, Nevada, Ogden, Perry, Spencer, Stanhope and Webster City.

Orphan trains brought thousands of children from New York City to the Midwest, including towns across Iowa. Farm families adopted many of these children. *Author's collection.*

Dorothy Urch, an orphan train rider who came to Algona, arrived in Iowa as Dorothy Brooks and was raised as Dorothy Johnson. "I was born in 1911 and arrived in Algona in February 1917 from the Children's Aid Society in New York City. I had come from a family of 10 kids, and I was the ninth. My father died when I was four, and Mother couldn't take care of all the younger kids. She didn't want us in an orphanage, though, so she gave us up to the Children's Aid Society."

Sometimes siblings on the orphan train were placed in the same home when they arrived in Iowa. This was the case for Clara Lickey and her older brother, Harry, who came to Woodburn in south-central Iowa in 1899 and lived with the J.W. Terhune family. "I have a horse, and I ride to Sunday school and I like to live on a farm," said Harry Lickey, who was ten years old when he wrote this letter, which is recorded in the *New York Juvenile Asylum Annual Report for The Year 1900* (volumes 48–52). "I help milk the cows, and I drive a team and plow and do all kinds of work on a farm and have finished husking corn, and I would not take anything for what I have learned this summer. I attend church, and our preacher talks very loud, but I like to hear him. Clara and I live together, and have a very nice home."

Little sister Clara was nine when she wrote to the orphanage in New York about her experiences near Woodburn:

> *I like to live on a farm. I have learned to ride horseback and to drive a team, and I can do most all kinds of work in the house. I go to church and Sunday school. We have two big ponds this summer, and we will have good times skating if Santa Claus brings us skates. Our guardians are very temperate and neither smoke, chew nor drink, nor will they allow card playing in the house. I have never seen a drunken man since I came to Iowa. Do tell the girls and boys in the asylum to come West if they want to have a good time. They will have lots of roast turkey and fried chicken and everything to eat. I have thirteen new dresses.*

While the Lickey children were placed in the same home, siblings on the orphan trains were often separated, since many couples only wanted one child, Harms said. This was the case with Dorothy Urch, who was five years old when she went to live with John and Carrie Johnson on their farm seven miles southeast of Algona. "My baby brother was sent to Kansas, and his family later moved to Canada," she said.

When asked about her years on the farm near Algona, Urch spoke highly of the Johnsons, a farm couple who adopted her in 1923. "They had a daughter who died when she was 13 months old, and they couldn't have more children. To be adopted is wonderful. My parents were fine Christian people."

Before Urch passed away at age ninety-six in 2007, she had given nearly two hundred talks about her orphan train experience and life on her family's Iowa farm to school groups, civic clubs and churches.

The orphan trains continued until 1929. Although the system had its pitfalls, the orphan trains and other Children's Aid initiatives led to a host of child welfare reforms, including child labor laws, adoption and the establishment of foster care services. "Much can be said for and against the orphan train method of obtaining homes and the upbringing of the child," Harms said. "But in Iowa, the rate of runaways was only 2 percent, and 85 percent of the matches were successful."

State Fair Is a Homecoming for Iowans

Then as now, being part of an Iowa farm family means living with the rhythm of the seasons. For generations, few events bring Iowa families together each summer like the state's county fairs (including Clay County's "World's Greatest County Fair," a Spencer tradition since 1918) and the great Iowa State Fair.

The internationally acclaimed Iowa State Fair in Des Moines is the single largest event Iowa. As one of the oldest and largest agricultural and industrial expositions in the country, the Iowa State Fair annually attracts more than 1 million people from all over the world each August. The Iowa State Fair is also the only fair listed in the *New York Times* best-selling travel book *1,000 Places to See Before You Die*. Domestic diva Martha Stewart even spent a day at the fair in 1999 to record segments for her hit television show.

While the first Iowa State Fair was held on October 25–27, 1854, in Fairfield, supported by a total operating budget of $323, the fair moved to its present location in 1886. "The state fair moved to this site in Des Moines after the State Legislature and the City of Des Moines appropriated funds to purchase Calvin and Arminta Thornton's farm," said Leo Landis, curator for the State Historical Society of Iowa. "One building original to the Thornton farm remains—Grandfather's Barn, which is on the far eastern edge of the fairgrounds."

By 1904, the Iowa State Fair showcased a new Agriculture Building, which was built along the route to and from the state fair from the Rock Island Railroad depot. Today, the Agriculture Building is home to the famous Butter Cow and other butter sculptures, which have been part of the Iowa State Fair since 1911.

J.K. Daniels sculpted the Iowa State Fair's first Butter Cow. Various "butter artists" carried on the tradition through the years, including Norma "Duffy" Lyon of Toledo, Iowa. She began sculpting in 1960, becoming the fourth person and first woman to sculpt the fair's butter beauties. In 2006, after fifteen years of apprenticing with Duffy, Sarah Pratt of West Des Moines became the fair's fifth butter sculptor.

The famous Butter Cow has been a big draw at the Iowa State Fair since 1911. Norma "Duffy" Lyon served as the fair's famed "Butter Cow Lady" for more than forty-five years. *Courtesy of the Iowa State Fair.*

The Butter Cow starts with a wood, metal, wire and steel mesh frame and about six hundred pounds of low-moisture, pure cream Iowa butter. Inside the forty-degree cooler, layers of butter are applied to the frame until a life-size butter cow emerges—measuring about five and a half feet high and eight feet long. Each year, much of the butter is recycled. The butter can be reused for up to ten years. The Butter Cow would butter about 19,200 slices of toast and take an average person two lifetimes to consume, according to the Iowa State Fair.

In addition to the Butter Cow, a companion sculpture also graces the Agriculture Building coolers each year during the fair. In 2018, a butter sculpture of the iconic Waterloo Boy Tractor stood next to the Butter Cow to celebrate John Deere's 100th anniversary of entering the tractor business. Other companion sculptures throughout the years have featured Iowa artist Grant Wood's famous *American Gothic* painting, Iowa native and Hollywood star John Wayne, Laura Ingalls Wilder (who lived in Burr Oak, Iowa, in the 1870s), a tribute to the famous Lincoln Highway (which runs across Iowa) and more.

The Iowa State Fairgrounds was listed in the National Register of Historic Places in 1987. "The Iowa State Fair connects generations of Iowans," said Iowa governor Kim Reynolds, who spoke during the opening ceremony of the 2017 Iowa State Fair. "There are so many wonderful memories and traditions here at the fair, which showcases the best of Iowa's agricultural and cultural heritage."

Chapter 8

HARD TIMES AND FARM REBELS

The culture of Iowa agriculture hasn't only been shaped by good times. The farm crisis that started in the 1920s, a decade before the Great Depression engulfed America, shook rural Iowa to its core. In the post–World War I era, the Golden Age of Agriculture was over, and farmers throughout the Midwest began to suffer the effects of an increasing economic depression that culminated at the close of the 1920s with the stock market crash.

"To understand the nature of the agricultural problem more clearly, it needs to be said that farming is a difficult and uncertain profession," noted Gary D. Dixon in his thesis "Harrison County, Iowa: Aspects of Life from 1920 to 1930," which he presented in 1997 to the Department of History to earn his Master of Arts degree from the University of Nebraska–Omaha. "The farmer has no control over the prices he pays for goods or, more importantly, for what he can ask for his own products, as he 'buys in a seller's market, and he sells in a buyer's market.'"

It was definitely a seller's market during World War I, when all sectors of the American economy produced as much as possible to help the war effort. It was profitable, as well as patriotic, to raise crops at top capacity. But then the war ended on November 11, 1918.

"Government price supports for agriculture were kept through 1920, when the guaranteed prices on wheat and other crops were terminated," Dixon noted. "The government ended loans to European nations at the same time, which meant they were unable to purchase U.S. agricultural products."

This is what had kept the exports going, and exports had driven the boom in the U.S. farm economy. In the years just after World War I, prices for farm goods fell by half, as did farmer income. The Federal Reserve raised the credit rate just when the farmer needed its help the most, so money tightened up. Banks did not renew notes, but mortgages and bills still came due. To make it worse, the railroads raised their freight rates, so it was more expensive to get the crops to market, Dixon noted.

Farm income fell from $17.7 billion in 1919 to $10.5 million in 1921—nearly a 41 percent drop. In Iowa, farm values that had almost tripled between 1910 and 1920 plunged during the 1920s. In Harrison County in southwest Iowa, 1930 land values of $41 million reflected a drop of more than $35 million from 1920, Dixon said. In addition, Harrison County's total crop values, which in 1919 were more than $10.8 million, fell to roughly $5.7 million by 1924. "Taxes on the remaining income, and the other expenses incurred in farming, remained as high as they ever were, or increased," Dixon added.

While there had been a historic growth in the number and size of farms in the nation until 1920, that soon changed. Then the farm population showed net losses of 478,000 in 1922 and 234,000 in 1923. The more lucrative prospects of the city lured many of the best of the younger generations away, Dixon said.

Banding Together in Farmer Cooperatives

In response to these troubling developments, some farmers began organizing with their neighbors so their shared concerns could be heard at the county, state and national level. Some turned to groups like the Iowa Farmers Union, which had formed in 1915 to help members work together to strengthen the independent family farm through education, legislation and cooperation.

Others turned to a new group, the Iowa Farm Bureau Federation (IFBF), which had formed on December 27, 1918, during a meeting in Marshalltown. Seventy-two county Farm Bureau groups from across Iowa voted unanimously during this meeting to form a state federation. These farmers knew that they needed a stronger voice in legislation governing their industry, improved marketing for their ag products and better relationships with other related industries, including meatpackers and the railroads.

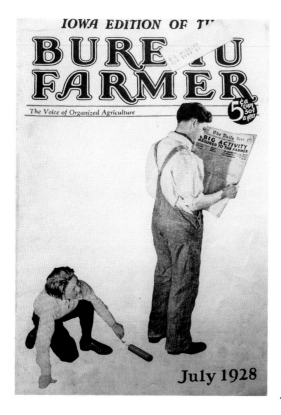

The Iowa Farm Bureau Federation formed in 1918. Members received the Iowa edition of the *Bureau Farmer* magazine, such as this one from July 1928. *Author's collection.*

"We regard this movement as one of the most sensible efforts toward an organization of farmers that has yet been made," said Henry A. Wallace, the editor of *Wallaces' Farmer*, who went on to become U.S. secretary of agriculture and vice president of the United States.

The IFBF also helped support the cooperative marketing movement that had been gaining momentum, noted Tim Neiss, IFBF historian. Ag cooperatives had started to form in Iowa by the mid-1800s in response to unfair business practices by the railroads that hurt competition and lowered the prices farmers received for their products. Farmers began banding together to market their products more efficiently, at higher prices, as well as to buy inputs at lower cost.

One of these early Iowa cooperatives was Farmers Cooperative Elevator of Marcus, which was incorporated on December 12, 1887. The Marcus location, which is now part of First Cooperative Association based in Cherokee, remains the oldest active cooperative elevator in the nation.

DESPERATE TIMES TRIGGERED FARMERS' HOLIDAY MOVEMENT

While establishing farm organizations and cooperatives appealed to some farmers, other farmers decided to move in a much more radical direction—one that would culminate in the Farmers' Holiday movement and the near-lynching of an Iowa judge.

By the time the stock market crashed in 1929, what bottom was left in the already weakened farm economy simply collapsed. While Iowa farms showed an average net income of $2,774 in 1929 (over $40,700 in today's dollars), the average net income in 1930 plunged to $763 (about $11,000 today), according to Rodney Carr from the University of Nebraska–Omaha, who wrote his thesis "The Farmers' Holiday Movement, Plymouth County, Iowa: 1932–1933" in 1980.

The farm debt situation took on crisis proportions by the early 1930s, especially when creditors started looking to recoup their financial losses by demanding repayment on agricultural loans. Country banks supplied most of the short-term credit to farmers. Iowa led the nation in bank failures from 1921 through 1931, with an average of eighty-seven per year, according to the article "The Struggle to Preserve Iowa's State Banking System, 1920–1933" in the winter 2001 issue of *The Annals of Iowa*.

Sometimes whole counties suffered during the banking crisis. Plymouth County experienced an almost total failure of its banking system in July 1932. Virtually every bank in the county closed around this time, Carr noted. The statewide banking crisis touched nearly every part of Iowa and left many citizens bankrupt, often overnight, as one bank after another closed its doors.

The Depression in the 1930s caused thousands of Iowa farmers to lose their farms due to foreclosures by banks and insurance companies. In 1925, fewer than twenty-five farms per thousand were foreclosed in Iowa. By 1932, that figure had doubled. In 1933, Iowa led the nation with seventy-eight foreclosures per thousand farms, Carr noted.

As foreclosures soared, angry Iowa farmers began fighting back, likely inspired by other strikes around the country. Truck drivers had gone on strike in Minneapolis. The "Bonus Army" marched in Washington, D.C., in March 1932. After victory in World War I, the U.S. government promised in 1924 that servicemen would receive a bonus for their service. The catch? The money wouldn't be paid until 1945. As the Great Depression dragged on, desperation motivated some of the veterans to protest in Washington, D.C., and demand their bonus right away.

This spirit of anger and protest also took root in rural Iowa. Some farmers joined the Farmers' Holiday Association, a statewide and national movement organized in 1932 by Iowan Milo Reno. The group was based on the idea that farmers were being treated unfairly by the current economic system, so farmers were urged to declare a "holiday" from farming.

Members believed that their economic fate could be changed if farmers were guaranteed prices that would cover their cost of production. If this cost of production standard were not met, Farmers' Holiday members would go on strike, withholding produce from the market until their demands were met. The Farmers' Holiday movement adopted the slogan of "Stay at Home—Buy Nothing—Sell Nothing."

The fact that Reno became the leader of his movement was no accident. Born in Wapello County near Agency, Iowa, in 1866, Reno had been raised by a family of Populists who supported political candidates who campaigned with promises to support the common people rather than the elites.

In 1918, he joined the Iowa Farmers Union (IFU) and was elected president of the Wapello County branch of the IFU in 1920. That same year, he was elected IFU state secretary/treasurer and led the fight to amend the IFU constitution "to secure for the farming industry cost of production plus a reasonable profit," according to the University of Iowa's online Biographical Dictionary of Iowa.

As IFU president during the 1920s, Reno worked to secure the cost of production for farmers. As the farm depression deepened, he organized direct action to improve prices. On May 3, 1932, thousands of farmers (some accounts mentioned two thousand farmers, while others put the number closer to three thousand) gathered in Des Moines to inaugurate the Farmers' Holiday Association. Reno became national president of the association. Their fight song became:

> *Let's call a Farmers' Holiday*
> *A Holiday let's hold*
> *We'll eat our wheat and ham and eggs*
> *And let them eat their gold.*

Normally conservative farmers soon employed strikes, roadside blockades and picketing. They interfered with legal proceedings. They even threatened lynchings. Nowhere was the activity of the Farmers' Holiday Association more intense than in northwestern Iowa. Plymouth County found itself in the epicenter of the farmers' violent revolt. Part of this was due to geography.

Roadblocks like this one organized near Sioux City in 1932 by the Farmers Holiday Association protested low prices paid for farmers' products. *Courtesy of State Historical Society of Iowa, Des Moines.*

Sioux City, with a population of about seventy-nine thousand in 1930, served as the major trade center and agricultural market for the tristate area of northwestern Iowa, southeastern South Dakota and northeastern Nebraska. Sioux City's grain terminals, stockyards and meatpacking plants made the city a key destination for the region's agricultural products.

U.S. Highway 75, a farm-to-market road, ran through Plymouth County to Sioux City. In the 1930s, this hard-surfaced road provided a key transportation route for agricultural products from numerous northwestern Iowa counties. In this geographic setting, the Farmers' Holiday Association achieved its most marked successes and failures.

The Farmers' Holiday Association planned to begin withholding ag products from the market starting on July 4, 1932. Because of organizational problems and temporary price gains in early July, the movement did not begin until August. Throughout the summer of 1932, Reno advocated direct action as he preached the virtues of a farm strike across Iowa. Other Farmers' Holiday Association leaders also traveled extensively across Iowa to promote the idea of a farm strike.

Boone County farmer Elmer Powers heard news of the impending strike on Saturday, August 6, 1932. "While we were eating dinner this noon, we heard a line ring on the phone," Powers wrote in his dairy, whose excerpts were later published in the book *Years of Struggle: The Farm Diary of Elmer G. Powers, 1931–1936.* "Listening, we learned the Farmers' Holiday or 'strike' was called for next Monday morning to begin at five o'clock."

The Farmers' Holiday Association officially began a movement to withhold agricultural products from the market on August 8, 1932. The focal point of the strike was Sioux City. "Today is the first day of the Holiday," Powers wrote on August 8. "Many farmers are very serious about it. All agree that it cannot make things much worse, and that something must be done."

On August 15, 1932, the *Sioux City Journal* reported hundreds of striking farmers blocking the highways to Sioux City, Carr noted. The largest group of strikers gathered at the Plymouth County line, with reports that no trucks carrying livestock or milk had been allowed to pass. Since this action was carried out by the milk producers and the Farmers' Holiday supporters, it was tough to determine who was leading the strike.

On August 19, the strike was on Powers's mind. "This afternoon we drove to the county seat. The lady of the farm marketed eggs, successfully 'running the blockade' the striking farmers had placed on the highway. We were able to do it while pickets were arguing with the driver of a truckload of ear corn."

Throughout mid-August 1932, more acts of rebellion broke out in Iowa. Two men poured out three hundred pounds of milk from a Cherokee Creamery truck, according to the *Sioux City Journal's* August 13, 1932 issue. At Kingsley, Iowa, farmers called on local grain elevators to quit buying farm produce and persuaded some farmers to return home with their grain. Also at Kingsley, farmers seized five milk trucks and planned to distribute the milk among the poor.

As the strike progressed, an illusion of success gripped farmers in the Sioux City area, Carr noted. On August 15, 1932, reports indicated that numerous Le Mars truckers had agreed not to haul agricultural products during the farmers' holiday. Three days later, the Le Mars Chamber of Commerce agreed not to buy produce for the duration of the strike.

Reports out of Sioux City indicated serious reductions in livestock receipts due to the strike. The news received national attention in the *New York Times* and other major newspapers. Although the farm strike gathered a great deal of media attention, the reality was that most farmers didn't participate, prompting radical members of the Farmers' Holiday Association to block roads to keep those still wanting to sell their goods from getting to the markets.

Although receipts had been drastically reduced at Sioux City, receipts at other midwestern livestock markets rose significantly. "The Farmers' Holiday effort at Sioux City was simply too limited in scope," Carr noted. "From late August on, disheartened by the news of failure, some farmers turned to more forceful and violent actions."

Trouble Erupts Near Council Bluffs

Roughly one hundred miles south of Le Mars, farmers attempted to blockade the Omaha markets in late August 1932. Picketers gathered on the north and east edges of Council Bluffs to stop incoming traffic trying to reach the markets, according to the Historical Society of Pottawattamie County (HSPC), Iowa. Sheriff Percy Lainson kept a watchful eye but allowed peaceful picketing. The peace didn't last, however.

Picketers blocked Highway 34 into town from the south and refused Deputy Frank Owens's order to not stand in the road. Ignoring the warning, picketers used telephone poles to block the highway near the Iowa School for the Deaf. Trees and road spikes were also used to block Highway 34, according to the February 2, 2014 Associated Press article "County Honors Special Deputy Killed in 1932."

Sheriff Lainson hired ninety-eight special deputies and promised "to fight it out if it takes 5,000 deputies," according to local news reports. "If the Pottawattamie County jail bulges with picketers, it will just have to bulge," he added. "I'm going to see that law and order are maintained."

Farm trucks attempting to deliver products to market were escorted through the strikers by armed deputies. Sheriff Lainson directed his deputies to arrest every man found picketing and charge him with unlawful assembly. As word spread that one thousand men were on their way to Council Bluffs to aid the picketers, the sheriff's force stood ready with submachine guns and riot guns.

Two truckloads of Plymouth County farmers joined the blockade effort in Pottawattamie County. Sheriff Lainson jailed a number of picketers, including four from Plymouth County. One of the picketers' leaders,

Raymond Snyder of Plymouth County, threatened Lainson that if the picketers were not freed, the farmers would storm the jail.

Tensions grew as reports swirled that men from out of town were said to be heading for Council Bluff's iconic Squirrel Cage jail (a three-story, revolving jail) to break the picketers out. Sheriff Lainson reported that if the jail were mobbed, his men were armed and would handle it "in the best possible manner." Deputies were authorized to shoot to kill, should any farmers try to storm the jail. The August 26, 1932 issue of the Council Bluffs' *Daily Nonpareil* newspaper published a front-page warning to citizens to stay away from the jail for their own safety, noted the HSPC.

Gunfire erupted, however, on Thursday, August 25, 1932. Claude Dail, a special deputy with just three days of service, was shot and killed when a gun accidentally discharged during a weapons test. Special Deputy Joe Ludwig was also injured.

Eventually, the Squirrel Cage jail's farmer-inmates were freed. While significant further violence was avoided, the picketing continued. Sheriff Lainson added fifty additional special deputies. Although strikes continued elsewhere, the situation at Council Bluffs was essentially over by late August 1932.

The depressed agricultural economic outlook and the increasing violence of the Farmers' Holiday movement prompted a hastily called governors' conference at Sioux City in early September 1932. Four midwestern governors attended the conference, which met on September 9–11. Milo Reno spoke for the Farmers' Holiday Association and recommended a debt moratorium. The governors submitted agricultural relief resolutions to President Herbert Hoover.

Farmers showed little faith in the entire proceedings, as picketers remained on Highway 75 near Sioux City. Then, as suddenly as the farm strike had materialized, it faded. By September 20, all roads into Sioux City were clear of pickets. Talk about resuming picketing in Plymouth County surfaced but did not materialize. Farmer activism temporarily disappeared, Carr noted. Perhaps the upcoming harvest season lured farmers back to their farms.

Whatever the reasons, the farm revolt quieted in Plymouth County until the winter and spring months, when it reemerged in a different form.

Farm Foreclosures and Penny Auctions

Rural radicalism in the early 1930s found powerful expression in the subverting of farm foreclosures and tax sales. The technique was simple: when a farm was foreclosed for overdue taxes or failure to meet mortgage payments, neighbors would show up at the auction and intimidate any potential buyers. Then the farm and equipment would be purchased at a token price and returned to the original owner. *Nation* magazine reporter Ferner Nuhn witnessed a so-called penny auction in Iowa and described this practice in March 1933: "A raw, chilly day. The yard of the farm, churned black in a previous thaw, is frozen now in ruts. There are 300 farmers here. The farmers are mostly middle-aged, very workaday in overalls, sagging sweaters, mud-stained boots."

These men were neighbors of the farmer who could no longer pay interest on a $2,000 mortgage. "These farmers have known him for years; they know

A large group gathered for this farm foreclosure sale in Iowa in the early 1930s. Police were on hand to keep farmers from preventing the auction from proceeding. *Courtesy of Library of Congress.*

he would pay if he could," Nuhn wrote. "Some of them know that soon their own property may be endangered by defaults."

After horses were offered for sale, machinery came next. "A hay rack, a wagon, two plows, a binder, rake, mower, disc-harrow, cultivator. A dollar, fifty cents, fifty cents, a quarter, a half a dollar. Sold to the farmer. His means of livelihood are saved to him."

LYNCHING A JUDGE

Startling violence erupted again in rural Iowa the spring of 1933. The flashpoint focused on District Court judge Charles C. Bradley, who announced on April 26 that he would hear cases objecting to the constitutionality of a debt moratorium law in Iowa. After five eastern insurance companies brought the suit that was to be heard on April 27, this triggered a mêlée that led to the demise of the local Farmers' Holiday Association movement.

A foreclosure sale was scheduled on the morning of April 27 at Primghar, Iowa. Some six hundred to one thousand farmers, many from Plymouth County, assembled to stop the sale. The foreclosure was not halted, but violence broke out as farmers rushed the few deputies present, took their clubs and forced them to kiss the American flag, Carr noted.

A group of farmers worked out an arrangement between creditor and debtor, according to an account in the May 3, 1933 issue of the *Iowa Union Farmer*. While the Modern 76ers, a council of O'Brien County farmers who negotiated foreclosure compromises, met in the courthouse, other farmers heard speeches outside. It was this crowd that provoked a fight that resulted in injuries to some of the farmers.

Frustrated by the events at Primghar and suffering a head wound from the fight, Morris Cope of Plymouth County told the crowd, "We'll go to Le Mars and get Judge Bradley."

A bit of background helps explain some of the rage that fueled Cope, a Kingsley-area farmer. His father, Jacob, had farmed 550 acres of excellent farmland, but on January 9, 1932, the elder Cope had 510 acres of mortgaged land foreclosed. By the planting season of 1932, he had been reduced to 40 acres of farmland because he could not meet mortgage and tax payments.

Jacob Cope had hoped to leave his 550 acres free and clear to his sons, but by 1932–33 there was little left for an inheritance. Jacob Cope witnessed much of his life's work lost in a few short years. His son Morris saw his hope for the future wiped out by the Great Depression. "His case was surely indicative of the desperation of activist farmers in Plymouth County," Carr wrote.

This desperation drove Morris Cope and a crowd of farmers to hunt down Judge Bradley on the afternoon of April 27, 1933. When the angry mob reached Le Mars, it held a rally at the local ballpark. The group made threats against the owners of Ed Durband's farm at Struble, north of Le Mars. Durband was behind in his rent payments and faced certain eviction from his farm.

While Plymouth County sheriff Ralph Rippey persuaded the group to disperse, many farmers moved on to the courthouse, where Judge Bradley was hearing opening arguments in the case challenging the Iowa moratorium law. The farmers surged into the courtroom and insisted that Bradley halt the hearing. The already irritated farmers were probably incensed when Bradley ordered them to remove their hats as he proclaimed, "This is my courtroom!"

When Judge Bradley refused to halt the proceedings, some of the farmers abducted him from the courtroom. They blindfolded Bradley, loaded him into a truck, took him about a mile southeast of Le Mars and threatened him with mutilation and hanging unless he agreed to stop signing mortgage foreclosures. A rope was thrown over the cross-member of a utility pole and placed around the judge's neck.

While some farmers tugged at the opposite end of the rope, others removed Bradley's trousers. R.F. Starzl, editor of the *Le Mars Globe-Post*, followed the farmers to the country and observed that "one gathered that this business was distasteful, to them, but they were impelled by some grim destiny that they could not resist. When the judge at last swore a sort of compromise oath, they all seemed relieved that they could retire with credit."

The mob dispersed and left the judge along the roadside. The near lynching of Judge Bradley received national attention in many major media outlets, including the *New York Times*. While farmer activism in northwest Iowa had received considerable attention prior to this, the wild events of April 27, 1933, caused the Farmers' Holiday Association in Plymouth County to lose many of its previous gains. "Popular support for reckless and illegal behavior could not be found," said Carr, who noted that Milo Reno, among others, deplored the incident involving Judge Bradley.

The official government reaction to the attempted lynching was swift and severe. Governor Herring proclaimed martial law in Plymouth and O'Brien

Counties on April 28, the day after the incident. By that afternoon, the first National Guard troops occupied Le Mars. Before the two-week martial law rule ended, more than one hundred men, mostly farmers from Plymouth County, had been arrested.

Support for the Farmers' Holiday movement in Plymouth County faded during the summer and fall of 1933. Some measure of economic relief came from the Roosevelt administration. The Agricultural Adjustment Act, an omnibus farm-relief bill, established the Agricultural Adjustment Administration in 1933.

In an attempt to control the hog supply, the Agricultural Adjustment Administration purchased more than 6 million animals at premium prices in the fall of 1933. The impact of the New Deal agricultural program was noticeable in Plymouth County, as farmers signed up for the corn-hog program. The Agricultural Adjustment Administration also announced plans to make corn loans available to farmers on October 25, 1933. The Agricultural Adjustment Act put a floor under commodity prices so farmers could service their debts.

FARMER COMES FACE-TO-FACE WITH BONNIE AND CLYDE

While the Farmers' Holiday movement passed into history, violence of another form erupted in rural Iowa in the summer of 1933 when the infamous Barrow Gang arrived in Dallas County. After a shootout with police on July 19, 1933, in Platte City, Missouri, the Barrow Gang was on the run and hid out on a wooded hilltop north of Dexter, overlooking the abandoned Dexfield Amusement Park.

Gang members included Bonnie Parker, Clyde Barrow, Buck Barrow (Clyde's older brother), Blanche Barrow (Buck's wife) and W.D. Jones. They spent four to five days in the area, recuperating from their wounds. Part of Buck's skull had been shot off, and Blanche had glass in her left eye.

When law enforcement officials heard that the Barrow Gang was camping near Dexfield Park, they formed a posse to raid the camp in the early dawn hours of July 24, 1933. After the shooting began, every member of the Barrow Gang was either wounded or dying.

While all this was going on, it was chore time at the nearby Feller farm. Nineteen-year-old Marvelle Feller (1913–2010); his father, Vallie; and their

When Marvelle Feller (1913–2010) was nineteen, he came face to face with outlaws Bonnie and Clyde on his family's farm during the early morning of July 24, 1933. *Author's collection.*

hired man were getting ready to milk the cows. The Fellers' police dog, Rex, alerted them to Clyde Barrow, who was armed and covered with blood. Clyde asked for help carrying Bonnie to the Feller family's 1929 Plymouth car. Marvelle had to show Clyde how to shift the gears, since all Clyde drove were Fords. "You'll be well repaid for this," said Clyde before speeding off.

Buck Barrow died at King's Daughter Hospital in Perry on July 29, 1933, due to injuries sustained during the shootout. His wife was taken into custody, convicted and sentenced to serve time at the Missouri State Penitentiary. While Bonnie, Clyde and W.D. Jones got away this time, Dexfield Park marked the beginning of the end. In less than a year, on May 23, 1934, Bonnie and Clyde were ambushed and killed in Louisiana.

Chapter 9

IOWA WOMEN BLAZE NEW TRAILS
IN AGRICULTURE

While women in rural Iowa haven't always made news headlines, they've played key roles in the development of Iowa agriculture from the state's earliest years.

Consider pioneer farmer Elmira Taylor. When her husband, Tarpley Taylor, planted corn in his Van Buren County, Iowa field in 1862, Elmira was right by his side. The book *Tarpleywick: A Century of Iowa Farming*, by Henry Taylor, details how Tarpley Taylor made a furrow with a single-shovel plow drawn by one horse. Elmira followed with a bag of seed corn and dropped two seeds with each step forward. When Tarpley had made one round, he used the same equipment to cover the seed by running a light furrow alongside the one in which the seed had been dropped. It was a slow process, no doubt.

Fast-forward to today, when one Iowa farmer with a sixteen-row planter seeding thirty-five thousand plants per acre can cover 260 to 300 acres per day. Sometimes it's a female farmer running the planter. What would Tarpley and Elmira think?

Jessie Field Shambaugh and the Birth of 4-H

Farm women also broke new ground in other ways in rural Iowa. Jessie Field Shambaugh (sister of the famous nursery and garden innovator Henry

Field) guided the formation of today's 4-H clubs during her tenure as a country schoolteacher in southwest Iowa.

At the turn of the twentieth century, "Miss Jessie" was a woman far ahead of her time. An innovative teacher, she introduced basic science classes in addition to the "Three Rs" in the country school curriculum. She believed in teaching country children in terms of country life and was a strong proponent of relating school lessons more closely to life on the farm and in the rural home.

In the spring of 1901, Miss Jessie's students at the Goldenrod School near Clarinda planted and tended a garden in the schoolyard. On alternate days after school, Miss Jessie met with the older boys to study corn production and met with the girls to discuss the art and science of homemaking. In the book *The Very Beginnings*, Miss Jessie (who was called "the Corn Lady" by her students) recalled that her ag lessons were simple because she had no lesson plans or scientific leaflets to rely on. "The eagerness and enthusiasm which was displayed by these groups in these after-school hours as I told them what

Jessie Field Shambaugh guided the formation of today's 4-H clubs during her tenure as an Iowa country school teacher. In the spring of 1901, Miss Jessie's students at the Goldenrod School near Clarinda tended a garden in the schoolyard. *Courtesy of Iowa Digital Library, University of Iowa.*

I knew about our main Iowa crop—corn—made me realize that here was a subject not in the school's curriculum, but one which was greatly needed in our vast agricultural area."

By developing the Boys' Corn Club and the Girls' Home Club, Miss Jessie created the forerunner of 4-H and became the first female ag teacher in the nation. Her knowledge of agriculture was extensive, as her father had encouraged her to learn about farming methods from the time she was a young girl. As early as age twelve, Miss Jessie attended local Farmers' Institute meetings with her father and listened to presentations from ag leaders like "Uncle Henry" Wallace, who edited *Wallaces' Farmer*.

Inspired by these ideas, Miss Jessie promoted hands-on, practical learning. She pioneered a powerful educational concept to help young people learn "to make the best better." By age twenty-four, Miss Jessie had been elected superintendent of schools for Page County. She was one of the first female county superintendents in Iowa.

Starting in 1906, she enlisted the assistance of the 130 one-room country schools in the county to form boys' and girls' clubs. Miss Jessie encouraged the young people to participate in judging contests. She believed that friendly competition inspired students to excel. At the Junior Exhibits held at the Farmers' Institute in Clarinda, entry classes for students included "Best 10 Ears of Yellow Dent Corn," "Best Device Made by a Boy for Use on the Farm" and "Best 10 Ears of Seed Corn Selected by a Girl."

The goal was to "make the country life as rewarding as it might be in any other walk of life," Miss Jessie noted in *The Very Beginnings*. "My mother always wanted to help the farm boys and girls," said Miss Jessie's daughter, Ruth Watkins of Clarinda, whom I interviewed in 2002. "She had great idealism and was able to carry it through to reality."

Women's contributions to the economic stability of their family's farms had always been tremendous, but their vital role producing food, preserving food, preparing meals, working in the field and more took on a new urgency during World War I, the Great Depression of the 1930s and World War II.

Women kept large gardens and orchards and dried or preserved the fruits and vegetables for use throughout the year. At hog butchering time, farm women canned meat, rendered lard and made sausage. They butchered poultry and gathered eggs for the family table. Farm women also baked bread, cakes, pies and cookies year-round.

Many helped milk cows, separated cream from the milk and churned butter for home use and for sale. Some also helped in the fields, from picking corn by hand to driving tractors and hauling grain.

Farm women have long played key roles on Iowa farms. Mary (Hawley) Bardole is shown here hauling grain in the 1940s on her family's farm near Rippey. *Courtesy Roy Bardole.*

Most women also made clothing for themselves and their children, often with fabric saved from cloth sacks that previously held livestock feed. They also washed, ironed and mended clothes for the whole family, including the hired man (or hired men) their husbands might employ. If that weren't enough, they were responsible for the care of children and the nursing of anyone in the household who was ill.

Women on more prosperous farms had hired girls to help them, and older daughters usually assisted their mothers as well. Many rural women faced the annual challenge of the March 1 moving day. Contracts between Iowa landowners and renters were renewed yearly on March 1. If the family had to move to a different farm, the move was never postponed, regardless of inclement weather or muddy roads.

Producing eggs and poultry became one of the primary ways women brought in cash in their family's farming operation, whether they rented or owned the farm. "While poultry raising was expected of farm women and was not usually considered a technically sophisticated enterprise, it actually entailed a high degree of skill," noted Dorothy Schwieder and Deborah Fink in their report "Iowa Farm Women in the 1930s," which was published in the winter 1989 edition of *The Annals of Iowa*. Women learned the trade first from their mothers and second from extension programs and farm journals. During the 1930s, *Wallaces' Farmer* had a regular feature, "The Poultry," which gave extensive information on poultry production.

In Dallas County, Iowa, Mrs. Harry Frakes, a poultry producer featured in *Wallaces' Farmer*, cleared $2,303.39 on her operation in 1931. (That equates to nearly $37,000 in today's money.) "She must have been an exceptionally good manager, and her 1,000 layers were several times the usual laying flock," Schwieder and Fink noted.

The usual marketing practice was to take eggs and poultry to town and trade them for groceries and dry goods. Merchants gave a slight bonus on eggs if the money were taken out in trade in their stores. Often, no money changed hands. The dealer merely kept a running account of a woman's balance.

Bridging the Town-Farm Divide

A trip to town no doubt reminded farm women of the 1930s just how drastically different their lives were from people who lived in Iowa's small towns and cities.

Cities and towns across America began connecting to the electric grid in the late 1880s and early 1890s. Residents in most rural towns in Iowa had municipal electrical service by the early 1900s. Many town families enjoyed electric lights, electric appliances and indoor plumbing—conveniences that were virtually nonexistent in most Iowa farmhouses.

At the same time, rural living was often portrayed in the press as dreary and monotonous. Advertisements in farm journals in the 1920s urged farm people to take the bleakness out of their lives by buying radios, self-contained lighting systems (promoted as a vast improvement from kerosene lamps) and other items that would "bring the city to the farm" and make city life a little less enticing for farm youth looking for opportunity.

A large advertisement from the Colt lighting company that ran in the March 11, 1921 edition of *Wallaces' Farmer* warned, "Don't blame your children if they decide that life on the farm is not worthwhile. Here is fair warning: every year thousands of young men and women, brought up on farms, move to the cities. In the cities they can find the comforts they demand. On the average farm they cannot. It's up to you to make your farm worth living."

The massive job of bringing electricity to rural America would require more resources than individual farmers could provide. In the depths of the Great Depression, President Franklin D. Roosevelt signed Executive Order No. 7037 in 1935 establishing the Rural Electrification Administration (REA). By 1936, the Rural Electrification Act had been passed and sparked a whole new era of rural electric cooperatives, where rural residents banded together to bring electricity to their farms.

This profound change ushered in a new era in Iowa farming. By some accounts, not even the telephone changed farm families' ways of living, thinking and acting as much as the coming of electricity. While not all farm families got rural electricity right away, the adoption was fairly swift. By the end of 1930s, 86,786 farm dwellings, or 40.7 percent of all farm dwellings in Iowa, were lit by electricity, noted Schwieder and Fink. Contrast that number with 21.4 percent in 1930 and 15.3 percent in 1920.

Even if all farm families did not have electricity by the end of the 1930s, at least with the passage of the Rural Electrification Act there was the promise of better days ahead.

In 1937, *Wallaces' Farmer* periodically ran articles about changes that occurred in farm homes after the electric power lines reached the farms. For an October 1937 article entitled "Servants on the Farm: Electricity in Rural Homes," the magazine asked farm women to share the ways they used electricity in their homes. The ones who responded all agreed that electricity was "the equivalent

Mrs. W.H. Helmke of Renwick used her new electric range shortly after the Helmke farm became the first farm in Iowa to be electrified by a rural electrification project. The Helmke dairy farm consumed nearly three hundred kilowatts of electricity per month. *Courtesy of Heartland Museum.*

of a houseful of servants—servants that carry water, sweep rugs, help with washing and ironing and preparing of meals."

The women stated that they used all types of electrical appliances, from washing machines to stoves to refrigerators. A farm woman from Tama County, Iowa, expressed her appreciation this way: "The good fairy, electricity, has waved her magic wand across my path and now I lead a charmed life....No water to be carried uphill; no waste water to be carried out; no kerosene lamps to be cleaned and filled; no hand-scorching sad irons to be used; no fuel to clutter up my kitchen in pails and boxes; no ashes to be swept up and carried out. It seems too good to be true."

The contrast—especially for Iowa farm women—from the days before rural electricity to the era of rural electricity can't be overstated. Many historians acknowledge that farm women bore the heaviest burden of daily life without electricity. "We are told to be more sociable," said an anonymous Iowa farm woman quoted in a 1915 U.S. Department of Agriculture bulletin called "Economic Needs of Farm Women." "Why, we can hardly find time to visit a neighbor and are too tired on Sunday for church. A good rest would be a more cheerful prospect than any picnic."

With the coming of electricity, a farm woman from Dallas County commented in a 1937 issue of *Wallaces' Farmer*, "The farm woman of

FROZEN baked goods, prepared ahead of the farming season, enable Mrs. Bill Block of Calhoun county to get away from her kitchen to help her husband with field work.

DINNER will bake while Mrs. Bill Block of Calhoun county helps her husband in the field. Automatic timer on the electric range will start baking at mid-morning, shut off when baking is completed. Cathy, 4, will go to grandmother's while her mother operates tractor.

by Wayne T. Messerly

Electric appliances free wife to . . .

Help in field

"When you see a man who's successful in his business, you can bet there's a good woman working with him."

You've often heard that statement, or something to the same effect. It's especially true in the farming business.

Count the number of tractor operators you see in the fields wearing head scarves snapping in the wind. And you'll have another reason why Iowa farmers are the world's biggest producers of food.

One of these head-scarf-wearing farm wives is Mrs. Bill Block of Calhoun county. She's often on a tractor seat, helping her husband with their 380-acre operation.

"Until they invent a tractor that can find its own way from the field to the farmyard, my wife is inexpendable!" declares Block, a

member of Calhoun County Electric Cooperative Association at Rockwell City.

"Last fall, she hauled in beans off of 30 acres in one day," Block adds. "We never could have harvested that much without help with the hauling."

Mrs. Block admits that she enjoys helping with farm work.

"But I wouldn't enjoy it nearly so much if my electric range, freezer and other electrical appliances didn't make it possible for me to keep my homemaking duties up to a satisfactory standard," she adds quickly.

"It's quite a satisfaction to be able to help whenever needed outdoors—and walk in after a morning in the wind and dust and take a piping hot meal from the oven," Mrs. Block says.

"When I'm on call to go help in

the fields, I can take baked goods from my freezer, all ready to put in the oven.

"I sometimes bake a pie while getting breakfast. And set the table before I go to the field," Mrs. Block explains.

"I prepare a roast with vegetables, a casserole, or whatever I want, put it in the oven of my electric range, set the timer to come on at the right time and shut off when the food is cooked. Then when we come in, a hot meal is ready to be taken from the oven. The electric coffee pot perks the coffee while we wash up. And there, you have it," Mrs. Block says.

"With my electric dryer, the laundry doesn't even pile up," Mrs. Block adds. "It is carrying on for me in this department while I'm outside."

Electricity, however, doesn't quite take care of the baby-sitting problem. So when Mrs. Block is working in the field, Cathy, age 4, usually goes to see her grandmother, Mrs. Ray Pearson, on a nearby farm. Michael, 9, and Jack, 6, usually are in school.

The Blocks have 220 acres in their home farm. And they rent an additional 160 acres. They feed out 150 to 200 head of cattle and about 100 hogs per year.

Carole Block of Rockwell City was featured in the *Iowa Rural Electric News* in the May 1961 article "Electric Appliances Free Wife to Help in the Field." *Courtesy Iowa Association of Electric Cooperatives.*

yesterday envied the city woman for her youthfulness. But now, with our modern homes, I think the city woman may well envy her farm sister."

Alvina Sellers Showcased Hats and Happiness

Through the years, rural Iowa has produced many dynamic, skilled, capable women, including Alvina Tesdahl Sellers, the famous "Hat Lady of Iowa." Whether she was speaking to area church groups or being interviewed on national television on *Late Night with David Letterman*, this farm wife from Clarion, Iowa, always left a big impression, thanks to her impeccable style and quick wit. "Letterman thought he had an easy target," Sellers said of her 1987 appearance on the popular late-night show. "An old lady from Iowa—with hats. I stood my ground during the interview."

Sellers's interest in collecting hats became a passion that lasted a lifetime and led to an outstanding, astounding collection of more than five thousand hats. "She [Alvina] always looked stunning, she always wore high heels," said Marlene Bartlett, a Rockwell, Iowa woman quoted in the June 3, 2003 *Mason City Globe Gazette* article "Hat Lady of Iowa—'Clarion's Greatest Ambassador Ever.'" "She was fabulous."

From a young age, Sellers had been inspired by her aunts, who were milliners in the area. Sellers's style was matched by her resilience. Raised on farm north of Holmes, Iowa, Sellers had to grow up fast after her mother, Anna Caroline, was killed in a tornado on June 9, 1927. Sellers, who was just eleven years old at the time, helped raise her two younger sisters and younger brother.

After Alvina graduated from Clarion High School in 1932, she married L.W. Sellers, a local farmer, in 1937. The couple raised their children, Sandra and James, on a farm south of Clarion. "My mother raised chickens, sold eggs and cream and helped in the field," noted her daughter, Sandra Sellers Hanson, who now lives in New York. "We all walked the corn and bean fields, hoeing weeds. My mother also helped my dad when the hogs got out."

In the early 1950s, Sellers and a friend started the Wall Lake Wee Women 4-H Club for girls who lived in their rural neighborhood. Sellers served as a 4-H leader for the next fifteen years, supported other 4-H activities in Wright County for many years and was inducted into to Iowa 4-H Hall of Fame in 2003.

After being named an Iowa Master Farm Homemaker in 1967, Sellers gave her first "Hats and Happiness" program, displaying hats from her extensive collection and sharing a story about each one. During the next thirty years, she refined her popular program, adding inspirational and humorous stories as she

Rural Iowa has produced many dynamic women, including Alvina Tesdahl Sellers of Clarion, the famous "Hat Lady of Iowa," whose collection included more than five thousand hats. *Courtesy of Heartland Museum.*

modeled each hat. The hats became metaphors for the lives of rural women interwoven with tales of family, faith, fun and good humor.

"I meet the most wonderful people in the whole world," Sellers said in a 1978 interview with the *Mason City Globe Gazette*. "And these people are sharing these old, old hats. They tell me to stop by, and they'll have a hat for me. So not only do I gain a hat, I gain a friend. Isn't that wonderful?"

Sellers presented her "Hats and Happiness" program 5,636 times for local, state and national organizations, from tiny country churches to giant auditoriums. "Dad supported Mother with everything she did," Hanson said. "They were partners in driving to her programs all over the country."

Today, hundreds of Sellers's gorgeous, colorful hats are housed at the Heartland Museum in Clarion. More than four hundred of Sellers's favorite, most spectacular hats are displayed in Alvina's Victorian Hat Parlor, where the story of this Iowa farm wife's amazing career is told in photographs and other artifacts.

There are hats of every shape, style, size and color imaginable, including holiday hats, designer hats from Saks Fifth Avenue in New York City, specialty shops in New Orleans and Iowa's famous Younkers department store in downtown Des Moines. Next to Alvina's Victorian Hat Parlor, Alvina's Millinery Shop contains her oldest and most elegant antique hats and bonnets. "A hat is a piece of magic," noted a publicity brochure from the Heartland Museum, which invites guests to "Come See Alvina's Hats."

As Sellers grew older, she remained resilient, always embodying poise and style. She stayed active in her community and church. She also retained her flair for the flamboyant and always wore a hat. While remaining a gracious, kind lady, Sellers gained a reputation for speaking her mind and encouraging people to think about their lives, choices and values.

Sellers celebrated during the local high school's homecoming every year—dressed in her own Clarion High School cheerleading outfit, of course. "That was Alvina," Barb Mussman, publisher of the *Wright County Monitor*, told the *Mason City Globe Gazette* in 2003.

When Sellers passed away on June 1, 2003, she left two legacies: her hats and her humor. "Alvina was the greatest ambassador Clarion ever had," Mussman said. "She did everything with enthusiasm and energy. She had a spirit that never quit."

INSPIRING GENERATIONS OF FARM LEADERS

Another north Iowan, Evelyn Latham, shared many similarities with Sellers. In the early 1960s, *Wallaces' Farmer* named Latham the Iowa Master Farm Homemaker of the Year. "My story is one of love and hard work, interspersed with joys, tragedies, achievements, and a lot of family pride," said Latham (1916–2014), who grew up on her family's farm near Latimer, taught in Franklin County's rural schools and played a key role in the Latham family's seed business for years.

Evelyn and her husband, Willard, founded Latham Seeds in Alexander, Iowa, in 1947. Willard Latham, a farmer and innovator, retrofitted a piece of equipment that helped clean and preserve oats against disease. Word spread to farmers in the area, and Latham Seeds was born. "Willard built a trailer to transport the equipment, and that was the beginning of our seed business," Evelyn Latham wrote in her memoirs. "He and John Hill went from farm to farm to clean oats that were full of weeds and infected with smut fungus disease. The men almost froze to death, so the next year Willard had farmers bring their oats to a shed on our farm, where the oats could be cleaned and treated."

Evelyn Latham ran the "office" in addition to raising the couple's five sons. "The family's kitchen table served as the company's office, so Evelyn made numerous trips daily from the house to the outbuildings whenever Willard needed to take a phone call," said Shannon Latham, who is married to Evelyn Latham's grandson John and serves as vice-president of Latham Hi-Tech Seeds. "Evelyn was known for her cooking skills and hospitality, and it wasn't unusual for her to feed a room full of hired men and customers."

Shannon Latham is glad that women like Evelyn paved the way for today's women in agriculture. "When I was in high school, my grandfather looked me in the eye and said, 'If you want to be a farmer, you'd better marry one.' Thanks to strong women in my life, I felt empowered to follow my dreams."

After graduating from Iowa State University (ISU) in May 1993 with a double major in agricultural journalism and public service and administration in agriculture, Latham became the director of legislative affairs for the Agribusiness Association of Iowa. Today, she not only serves as vice-president of Latham Hi-Tech Seeds, but she also owns and operates a pumpkin patch and agritourism destination, Enchanted Acres, near Sheffield in northern Iowa. "I'm able to pursue my passions and advocate for agriculture," said Latham, who also enjoys cooking and shared this recipe from Grandma Evelyn Latham's recipe box:

Ice Cream Dessert
2 cups crisped rice cereal
1 cup shredded coconut
½ cup chopped nuts of your choice
⅔ cup packed brown sugar
⅓ cup butter, melted
½ gallon vanilla ice cream (softened)

Crush rice cereal with rolling pin; then mix cereal with coconut, nuts, brown sugar and butter. Pat two-thirds of this mixture in the bottom of a 9-inch by 13-inch cake pan. Spread softened ice cream on top. Sprinkle remaining cereal mixture on top. Freeze.

Tragedy Drove Marilyn Adams to Create Farm Safety 4 Just Kids

As Latham and Sellers knew, farming and motherhood can be some of the toughest jobs in the world. Marilyn Adams certainly understood. Her story revolved around a bright October day in 1986, when harvest was just beginning in Iowa. Her eleven-year-old son, Keith, was excited to stay home from school to help on the farm. A mature, responsible kid, Keith was given the task of watching the gravity-flow wagon being filled with corn. What should have been a productive time on that glorious fall day turned deadly, however, when Keith fell into the wagon. He was quickly sucked down into the load of corn, where he suffocated.

How did this happen? When grain flows, it forms a funnel, with the wide mouth of the funnel at the top and a smaller opening at the bottom. If you're in a wagon or grain bin when the grain is flowing, you can quickly become engulfed in grain. Depending on the size of the auger moving the grain, you can be trapped in grain up to your waist within ten seconds and completely submerged within twenty-five seconds. Once you're submerged in grain, it can take more than one thousand pounds of force to free your body, according to Penn State University Extension.

After "nearly a year of sobbing on the bed" following Keith's death, Adams said that her daughter unintentionally handed her a mission. Kelly had joined Future Farmers of America (FFA) and wanted to give a speech on the dangers of gravity-flow wagons. She enlisted her mother's help with the research, noted the 2016 *Iowa Farm Bureau Spokesman* article "Iowa Advocate Sees Progress in Farm Safety Awareness." That grew into a project to put danger decals on gravity-flow wagons. "From there, we researched one safety threat after another and developed an educational program around it," Adams said.

This inspired Adams to create the nonprofit organization Farm Safety 4 Just Kids (FS4JK) in Earlham, Iowa, in 1987. At that time, there were few or no farm safety programs for kids. Adams wanted to prevent other families from experiencing a tragedy like the one her family had.

By the time FS4JK celebrated its twenty-fifth anniversary in 2012, the organization had promoted farm safety to more than 6 million people through a network of more than 120 FS4JK chapters across the United States and Canada. "I didn't really know what to expect when I started FS4JK," Adams said at the anniversary. "The organization has grown and evolved so much. It's exciting to think about what lies ahead for the farm safety movement."

In the past thirty years, the number of kids killed each year in farm accidents has decreased from around three hundred per year to around one hundred, noted the 2016 *Spokesman* article. "But the true impact may be more than just numbers," the article continued. "Farm safety awareness is now entrenched in ag production and education. FFA and 4-H projects incorporate farm safety. Ag industries include safety in policies and procedures. Enhanced safety has driven farm equipment design."

Yet there's still work to do. When FS4JK dissolved in 2016, it donated its resources to the Progressive Agriculture Foundation, which teaches farm and home safety to kids. Thanks to Adams's courage to rise above adversity and reach out to others, a commitment to farm safety remains alive and well in rural Iowa.

Wire and Pliers: NASA Astronaut Peggy Whitson Shares Farm Lessons

While farm women like Adams charted a new course in rural Iowa, others like Dr. Peggy Whitson reached for the stars. Whitson knows what it's like to be in orbit with the International Space Station and to take a spacewalk.

"Stargazing is amazing," said Whitson, an astronaut who recently retired from the National Aeronautics and Space Administration (NASA). Seeing different-colored soils on Earth's farming regions is spectacular. But bringing some practical farm know-how along for the ride is also essential. "I was lucky to grow up on a farm," said Whitson, a southern Iowa native from Beaconsfield (population thirty-two during Whitson's youth). "Dad said you could fix almost anything with no. 2 wire and pliers. Guess what? I got to use my 'wires and pliers' skills in orbit."

When she spoke at the Iowa Farm Bureau Federation's annual meeting in December 2018, Whitson described a time when a panel in a solar array tore in space. "We had to take the tension off the tear so we could continue [the mission]," said Whitson, as she addressed hundreds of farmers in the ballroom of the Community Choice Credit Union Convention Center in downtown Des Moines. "There's no Lowe's store up there, so we had to fix it ourselves with the tools we had."

The "wires and pliers" solution worked, and that solar array is still in space, producing 97 percent of its power. This example reminded Whitson of the many practical lessons she learned growing up in rural Ringgold County. "On the farm, you couldn't always expect someone else to solve a problem when something failed or broke," said Whitson, who was inducted into the Iowa Aviation Hall of Fame in 2011 and named to *Time* magazine's 100 Most Influential People list in 2018. "You might not have time to go to town to get a replacement part. You have to adapt, just like you do in space."

Whitson's unique ability to remain rooted in the farm while reaching for the stars started at age nine, when she and millions of other Americans turned on the television to watch Neil Armstrong and Buzz Aldrin land the Apollo 11 Eagle lunar module on the moon on July 20, 1969. "Watching them walk on the moon was so impactful for me," said Whitson, who has participated in ten spacewalks. "'Holy cow!' I thought. 'What a cool job!'"

Fast-forward to 1978. Whitson graduated from high school in Mount Ayr that year, and Sally Ride became one of the first women selected when NASA recruited women to become astronauts for a spacecraft that had not yet flown: the Space Shuttle.

Inspired by science-related career options, Whitson earned her bachelor's degree in biology/chemistry in 1981 from Iowa Wesleyan College in Mount Pleasant, followed by a doctorate in biochemistry from Rice University in Texas in 1985.

After serving as an adjunct assistant professor at Rice University in biochemical and genetic engineering, Whitson joined NASA in 1989 as a research biochemist. By April 1996, she had been selected as an astronaut candidate and began training in August 1996. "Those two years of basic training were challenging," said Whitson, who studied orbital mechanics and more.

In 2002, Whitson became NASA's first Space Station science officer. By 2008, she was named the first female commander of the International Space Station. Throughout her distinguished career, Whitson completed more than fifty missions and broke many barriers. She claimed the title for most spacewalks for a woman. With a total of 665 days in space, Whitson holds a record—more time living and working in space than any other American or any woman worldwide, plus she places eighth on the all-time space endurance list, according to NASA.

NASA astronaut Peggy Whitson grew up on a farm near Beaconsfield. She shared her story during the Iowa Farm Bureau Federation's annual meeting in Des Moines in 2018. *Author's collection.*

"Set your goals high, but also enjoy the journey of getting there," advised Whitson, who almost single-handedly redefined the role of women in space exploration.

Val Plagge Helps Rural, Urban Residents Find Common Ground

Iowa farm women aren't afraid to dream big while staying grounded. Taking care of the land is a priority for Valerie (Val) Plagge and her husband, Ian, who farm near Latimer in north-central Iowa. "We raise corn, soybeans, pigs and kids," said Val Plagge, who maintains farm records, helps with field work, advises her husband on farm marketing opportunities and cares for the couple's most important "crop," their four children.

"I live by the saying, 'Bloom where you are planted,'" Plagge said. "I'm proud to be a farmer, a farmer's wife and a stay-at-home mom. Combine that passion with my love for my community and volunteering, and there always seem to be fields of opportunities for my family and me in rural north Iowa."

In 2012, Plagge started her blog *Corn, Soybeans, Pigs and Kids* to share stories of her family and their farm. Her posts also address timely agricultural issues and food trends. "This blog has been an excellent way to keep our landlords up to date on happenings around the farm, plus it's an outreach tool for consumers," Plagge said.

The blog has opened up speaking opportunities, media interviews and more for Plagge, who has spoken on a farmer panel at the Smithsonian in Washington, D.C., to address agricultural issues.

More opportunities have come through Plagge's volunteer work with CommonGround, where women in agriculture share their daily experiences on the farm, along with relevant science and research, to help build trust find common ground with consumers.

"It's based on the idea that we need to make food and farming personal," said Plagge, who noted that CommonGround is a partnership between the Iowa Corn Growers Association, the Iowa Soybean Association, the National Corn Growers Association and the United Soybean Board. "As consumers get further away from the farm, the more questions they have about the food they feed their families. By having these conversations, I want to help people sort through the myths and misinformation surrounding agriculture and show how real families like ours raise food for your family."

Eco-friendly farming is important to the Plagges, as they look for ways to protect the environment. To enhance soil conservation, the Plagges have changed their tillage practices to include no-till soybeans and minimal tillage in their cornfields. This also has reduced the number of trips across the field, which means reduced fuel consumption and less soil compaction.

Ian and Val Plagge own a feeder-to-finish hog operation and a row-crop farm near Latimer in north-central Iowa, where they are raising their children Klayton, eight; Audrey, six; Lauren, five; and Reagan, three (ages at time of publication). *Courtesy of Val Plagge.*

The Plagges also work with a nutrient management specialist to create manure management plans for their swine operation. These plans help ensure the family's crops receive proper amounts of fertilizer. The Plagges take soil samples and have a laboratory test the samples to determine which parts of their fields need more nutrients and which have enough. This data helps them determine the best places to apply swine manure without overapplying nutrients. All this helps protect soil and water quality.

This attention to detail hasn't gone unnoticed. The Plagges received the Iowa Farm Bureau Federation's 2016 Young Farmer Achievement Award and were inducted into the Outstanding Farmers of America in 2018.

In addition to running the farm operation, the Plagges are active members of their community, volunteering with their church, 4-H, the Make-A-Wish-Foundation and other organizations. "My family is at the heart of everything I do," Plagge said. "They motivate me to be the best wife, mom and role model possible."

Chapter 10

IOWA'S AG INNOVATORS

W hen Apple Inc. debuted its iconic "Think different" television commercial on September 28, 1997, the message, narrated by Richard Dreyfus, captured the public's imagination:

> *Here's to the crazy ones, the misfits, the rebels, the troublemakers, the round pegs in the square holes…the ones who see things differently—they're not fond of rules.…You can quote them, disagree with them, glorify or vilify them, but the only thing you can't do is ignore them, because they change things…they push the human race forward, and while some may see them as the crazy ones, we see genius, because the ones who are crazy enough to think that they can change the world, are the ones who do.*

Call them crazy or call them visionaries, but talented, hardworking entrepreneurs have advanced Iowa agriculture for generations, all in the quest to find better ways to farm.

FARMING SMARTER, NOT HARDER: THE LOUDEN MACHINERY COMPANY STORY

If you know where to look, many of Iowa's iconic barns that are still standing can tell stories of ag innovation and homegrown success—due, in part, to an

Iowa entrepreneur who never gave up, even when all the odds were against him. Farming would not be the same today without the contributions of William Louden and the Louden Machinery Company of Fairfield in southeast Iowa.

It has been said that Louden's contributions to barns and modern livestock farming were as revolutionary as what John Deere did for plows and Cyrus McCormick did for grain reapers. Louden's first patent in the 1860s focused on a labor-saving hay-stacking device, followed by the first patented manure carrier and other innovations to make work in the barn quicker and easier. The impact of this innovation reached far beyond the farm. The basic principles of Louden's material-carrying system would be adapted to help America win World War II and contribute to the National Aeronautics and Space Administration's Apollo space program in the 1960s.

"William Louden has come to be a recognized authority throughout the country on the subject of barn equipment and the care of cattle and other stock," as noted in *History of Jefferson County, Iowa*, published in 1912. "His methods have shown that the value of a milk-producing animal may be greatly enhanced by proper care."

Louden was born on October 16, 1841, in Cassville, Pennsylvania. His parents, Andrew and Jane Louden, both Irish immigrants, moved to the Fairfield, Iowa area when Louden was six months old. Louden spent his youth attending country school (and later Axline University in Fairfield), in addition to working on the farm when he could. Young Louden often suffered from bouts of illness, including a nearly fatal case of inflammatory rheumatism in his early twenties. Due to his health issues, he set his mind on devising ways to make farm work easier.

After watching others pitch hay from a wagon into a barn by hand, Louden devised a mechanism he called a hay carrier to make this job easier. He produced this first hay carrier in a little shop on his father's farm. With its system of pulleys, rope and a trolley that ran on a track in the roof of the barn, the labor-saving hay carrier made it more efficient to move hay from a wagon and stack it in the barn. On September 24, 1867, Louden received his first patent. This hay-stacking system was the first device of its kind to be patented in the United States.

Louden assembled a number of these new hay carriers on his family's farm (known as Loudendale) south of Fairfield. He traveled the countryside trying to sell them. He would install the mechanism in a barn so the farmer could try it. As he continued to refine his inventions, Louden opened his first factory around 1870–71 in Fairfield.

This marked a bold leap of faith, especially in this era. "It was a serious undertaking for a green country boy in a pioneer community where there were no manufacturing facilities, and where the thought of the people ran in an entirely different direction," according to *History of Jefferson County, Iowa*. "In these old pioneer days, brawn and muscle were relied upon to win, and one who tried to find an easier way to do things was not generally considered with favor. He was most frequently looked upon as lazy or trifling, and as trying to shirk his part of the work."

In time, farmers saw the advantage of these various innovations, including the hay carrier, and began to build barns accordingly. Besides easing the backbreaking labor that defined nineteenth-century farms, Louden's inventions triggered radical changes in barn designs. As more farmers began to use hay carriers, barns could be built bigger and taller, enabling farms to become larger and more efficient. Now that farmers could store more hay, they could keep more livestock through the winter.

Louden saw an opportunity to help famers by offering free barn planning services. "Many farmers owe the good construction and convenience of their barns to the barn-planning service which he [Louden] established and made free to all who needed it," wrote *Country Gentleman* magazine in 1932. These plans included the most up-to-date innovations, including manure/litter carriers to save labor; cupolas to help remove moisture and provide fresh air, thus improving animal health; and cork brick floors to prevent leg injuries among animals that were confined for long periods of time.

In 1907, Louden Machinery Company began offering a free barn planning service to help farmers construct more efficient barns (designed to use Louden barn equipment, of course). Some of this heritage is still on display locally at the historic Maasdam barns near Fairfield.

By 1939, more than twenty-five thousand original Louden barn plans had been distributed all around the world. Tens of thousands of additional barns were equipped or retrofitted with Louden products.

When Louden died on November 5, 1931, at age ninety, his company held 118 patents, according to the Biographical Dictionary of Iowa. One of the most unique patents focused on a manure removal system whereby a metal carrier was suspended from a rail system attached to the barn ceiling. Manure could be scooped into the large metal carrier, which could be moved throughout the barn, via the ceiling-mounted rail, and easily dumped outside. This patent allowed the Louden Company to expand into material handling systems that would eventually be used by factories all over the country, enabling Louden's legacy of agricultural labor-saving devices to carry over into modern American industry in the early twentieth century.

By World War I, manufacturers had begun to see that the concept behind Louden's monorail overhead traveling crane system for manure removal in barns could speed up production and save money. Louden's reputation for innovation, reliability and quality allowed the firm to expand into this new market opportunity. Soon this division became predominant at the Louden Machinery Company.

During World War II, two major manufacturers used Louden material handling equipment. Boeing integrated these systems in its B-29 airplane plants. The Louden Machinery Company was also chosen to construct material handling devices for the manufacture of atomic bombs in Oak Ridge, Tennessee. Members of the Louden family continued to run the company until 1953, when they sold it to Mechanical Handling Systems Inc. (MHS). In the 1960s, Louden built twenty-seven cranes and other devices to handle NASA's Apollo space booster rocket at Huntsville, Alabama, including two miles of track. At the height of the Cold War, the company also supplied overhead cranes in 1961 for a Boeing plant in Wichita, Kansas, that assembled B-52H airplanes, according to "The Louden Machinery Company Story" on the Jefferson County, Iowa website.

In 1965, MHS discontinued the manufacture of farm products. Louden's sterling reputation for high-quality material handling equipment will be forever linked, however, with Fairfield and Iowa's ag history.

GEORGE WASHINGTON CARVER ROSE FROM SLAVERY TO SCIENTIST

A man who was born a slave changed the world with his agricultural innovations, and the seeds for these contributions were planted in Iowa. George Washington Carver was not only the first black student and first black faculty member at Iowa State College, but he also became one of the nation's great educators, agricultural researchers and humanitarians who left a lasting legacy in Iowa and beyond.

Carver's journey began on a southwest Missouri farm owned by Moses and Susan Carver near the town of Diamond. It's uncertain whether Carver was born in 1864 or 1865. Both of his parents had been enslaved. His father died around the time of his birth. His mother, Mary, was given her freedom by the Carvers, and she adopted their last name.

The Carvers eventually took young George into their home and raised him as their own. He was unusually talented at almost everything he tried to do. By the time he was a teenager, Carver had left the farm to attend a school for black children in Neosho, Missouri. For the next ten years, Carver wandered from town to town in Missouri and Kansas in search of a better education. He supported himself by taking in laundry and doing household chores, according to Iowa Pathways, an online learning environment from Iowa PBS.

"From a child, I had an inordinate desire for knowledge and especially music, painting, flowers, and the sciences, algebra being one of my favorite studies," Carver wrote. "I wanted to know the name of every stone and flower and insect and bird and beast. I wanted to know where it got its color, where it got its life—but there was no one to tell me."

Carver was accepted at Highland College in Kansas, only to be turned away shortly after he arrived by school officials who were surprised by his skin color. Undeterred, he set off for Iowa, where he arrived in Winterset in 1888. This county seat town in Madison County was located along a section of the Underground Railroad that had been a hotbed of activity from 1857 through 1862, according to the Madison County Historic Preservation Commission.

While Carver found work as a hotel cook in Winterset, he wanted to be an artist—a painter—and capture the beauty of nature that so fascinated him. Friends in Winterset recognized his talents and encouraged him to enroll at Simpson College in Indianola, Iowa, where he studied art and music. It took only a few months for his art teacher, Etta Budd, to realize that she had nothing else to teach the talented young man. At her urging, Carver transferred in 1891 to Iowa State College in Ames, where her father was the head of the Department of Horticulture.

Through quiet determination and perseverance, Carver excelled at his studies and became involved in all facets of campus life in Ames. He was an active participant in debating and agricultural societies and the Young Men's Christian Association (YMCA). He was also a trainer for athletic teams (including Iowa State's football team), captain of the campus military regiment and a dining room employee, according to Iowa State University (ISU). His poetry was published in the student newspaper, and his artwork was exhibited at the 1893 World's Fair in Chicago.

Carver earned his bachelor's degree in 1894. "Reading about nature is fine, but if a person walks in the woods and listens carefully, he can learn

George Washington Carver was born into slavery and became Iowa State's first African American student, graduate and faculty member. Carver was a genius at finding new uses for agricultural commodities. *Courtesy of Iowa State University.*

more than what is in books, for they speak with the voice of God," Carver said. His professor, Dr. Louis Pammel, encouraged him to stay at Iowa State and pursue a graduate degree. Because of his proficiency in plant breeding, Caver was asked to join the faculty. Not only did he become the first black student at the school to earn a master's degree (in 1896), but he also became Iowa State's first black faculty member, all while expanding his knowledge and skills and writing professional papers of national acclaim.

Carver planned to earn his doctorate at Iowa State, and the school wanted very much to keep him on its faculty. But then a letter arrived in 1896 that changed everything. "I cannot offer you money, position, or fame," it said. "The first two you have. The last, from the place you now occupy, you will no doubt achieve. These things I now ask you to give up. I offer you in their place work—hard, hard work—the task of bringing a people from degradation, poverty and waste to full manhood." It was signed by Booker T. Washington, the principal of an industrial and teacher training institute for black students in Tuskegee, Alabama.

Washington was determined to make the Tuskegee Institute the leading black educational institution in the South. He wanted to establish an agriculture department. There were 5 million black farmers in the South. Most lived in poverty and ignorance of scientific agriculture. But to establish such a department, Washington knew that he needed a black man with an advanced degree in agriculture. There was only one such man in America: George Washington Carver.

Carver accepted Washington's offer. This opportunity to serve fit with Carver's philosophy that "education is the key to unlock the golden door of freedom." Carver urged southern farmers to rotate crops and use organic fertilizers. He preached the value of planting soil-restoring crops such as peanuts, sweet potatoes and soybeans.

At Tuskegee, Carver gained an international reputation in research, teaching and outreach. His research resulted in the creation of more than 300 products from peanuts, more than 150 uses for sweet potatoes and multiple uses for soybeans. These products contributed to rural economic improvement by offering alternative crops to cotton that were beneficial for the farmers and for the land.

"Anything will give up its secrets if you love it enough," Carver wrote. "Not only have I found that when I talk to the little flower or to the little peanut they will give up their secrets, but I have found that when I silently commune with people, they give up their secrets also—if you love them enough."

Some of Carver's most interesting, plant-based innovations included diesel fuel, axle grease, hand cleaner, stains and paints, gasoline, glue, insecticide, linoleum, printer's ink, plastics, laundry soap, medicines and more.

During World War I, Carver worked with the U.S. Department of Agriculture (USDA) as a consultant on food and nutrition. Carver had risen to fame nationwide by the 1920s and 1930s, thanks to his agricultural pursuits. By the early 1940s, Carver was working with Henry Ford, founder of Ford Motor Company, who supported the production of ethanol as an alternative fuel and showcased a car with a lightweight plastic body made from soybeans.

Carver remained at Tuskegee until his death in 1943. Landmarks across the nation have been named in honor of Carver, including the George Washington Carver Center on the USDA campus in Beltsville, Maryland. In Iowa, Carver's legacy is celebrated at Iowa State University, where Carver Hall was named in his honor. Through the George Washington Carver (GWC) Scholarship program, the university awards one hundred scholarships in the amount of tuition to multicultural, first-year students coming to college directly out of high school.

"It is not the style of clothes one wears, neither the kind of automobile one drives, nor the amount of money one has in the bank, that counts," Carver wrote. "These mean nothing. It is simply service that measures success."

Henry A. Wallace: Hybrid Corn Pioneer

While Iowa has been blessed with many talented agriculturists, perhaps none contributed as much, in so many different capacities, as Henry A. Wallace. His impressive résumé included stints as editor of *Wallaces' Farmer* (1921–33), founder of the Pioneer Hi-Bred Corn Company (1926), U.S. secretary of agriculture (1933–40), U.S. vice president (1941–44), U.S. secretary of commerce (1945–46) and U.S. presidential candidate (1948).

"Henry A. Wallace, more than any other single individual, introduced hybrid corn to the American farmer and fervently promoted its adoption," wrote William Brown in his article "H.A. Wallace and the Development of Hybrid Corn" in the fall 1983 edition of *The Annals of Iowa*. "The advantages of hybrid corn over the open-pollinated varieties in use in the early 1900s were so great that eventually hybrids would have caught the fancy of even the most conservative farmers."

Henry A. Wallace was born on the family farm in 1888 in Adair County in southwest Iowa near Orient. He was the third generation of a family of prominent Iowa agricultural leaders. His paternal grandfather "Uncle Henry" Wallace was a minister turned farmer, speaker and writer in southwest Iowa who valued the role that livestock and crop rotation played in maintaining soil fertility.

Uncle Henry and his son, Henry C. Wallace, purchased a weekly publication that would eventually become *Wallaces' Farmer*. Henry C. Wallace's decision to move his family from the farm near Orient to Ames in 1892 so he could complete his college degree and become an associate professor of dairy science at Iowa State College would have life-changing implications for his son, Henry A. Wallace.

Long before he became interested in hybrid corn, Henry A. Wallace was fascinated by the study of plants. George Washington Carver, a botanist at Iowa State College and friend of the Wallace family, sometimes took young Henry A. Wallace with him when collecting plant specimens. "I had great affection for him [Carver], simply because he was patient," Wallace wrote years later.

In 1896, the family moved to Des Moines, Iowa, when *Wallaces' Farmer* began publishing weekly. Henry A. Wallace earned high marks at Des Moines's West High School, exceling in German, Roman history, algebra, English, physiology and American history. He also started taking college-level courses in high school, which further fueled his interest in corn. He was inspired by the corn evangelist Perry G. Holden, an agronomy professor at Iowa State.

Four generations of the Wallace family are shown here, including (*clockwise from top*) Henry C. Wallace, "Uncle Henry" Wallace, Henry Browne (H.B.) Wallace (born in 1915) and Henry A. Wallace. *Courtesy of Iowa State University.*

Sixteen-year-old Henry A. Wallace attended one of Holden's short courses in 1904, Brown said. Although he questioned the value of the "beauty contest" in predicting yield potential by the corn's appearance only, he felt that careful observation of corn permitted a better understanding of the plant.

Also, the short-course instructor encouraged Wallace to plant forty ears on an ear-to-row basis the next season and compare yields, according to the Wallace Centers of Iowa. Wallace grew his first experimental plot in Des Moines while still a high school student. He found that the ear that had placed first in the corn show yielded among the poorest. "This was the start of his life-long involvement with the improvement of corn through genetic selection," noted the Wallace Centers of Iowa.

SPREADING THE HYBRID CORN MESSAGE THROUGH *WALLACES' FARMER*

After Henry A. Wallace graduated from West High in Des Moines in 1906, he attended Iowa State College, began writing for *Wallaces' Farmer* and continued his experiments with corn. After college graduation in 1910, he went to work full-time for *Wallaces' Farmer*, where he published a series of articles related to hybrid corn.

One of the first things that plant scientists like Wallace noticed when they began crossing different pure lines of corn was that hybrid plants were usually more vigorous than their parents. The simple act of crossing different strains resulted in higher yields and stronger plants—hybrid vigor. A fall 1992 issue of *TIME* magazine declared the hybridization of corn to be one of mankind's greatest achievements of the last one thousand years, noted Steve Kenkel, a farmer, hybrid corn collector and historian from Earling in southwest Iowa.

As Wallace envisioned the possibilities for higher-yielding hybrid corn, he lamented about woefully inadequate supplies of hybrid corn seed. With the help of a few friends, Wallace organized the Hi-Bred Corn Company (later known as Pioneer Hi-Bred and now Corteva Agriscience™), which was incorporated in Iowa on April 20, 1926.

Within a few years, Wallace struck a deal with Roswell Garst of Coon Rapids, Iowa, to help promote hybrid corn in Iowa. Garst, a salesman extraordinaire, convinced cash-poor Iowa farmers to purchase this new product during the Great Depression. "It wasn't easy to sell hybrid corn when my grandfather started in 1930," said Liz Garst of Coon Rapids.

Like their fathers and grandfathers before them, Iowa farmers saved their own seed and used fertilizer from the manure of their livestock. "When my grandfather would show up selling hybrid corn in peck bags for eight dollars each, the farmers would sneer in disbelief," Garst noted.

An undeterred Roswell, who was famous for putting his feet on farm wives' kitchen tables as he visited with their husbands, would urge the farmer not to pay him eight dollars. "Instead he'd tell the farmer to take a bag of seed and plant it side by side with open-pollinated corn," Garst added. "Then Roswell said he'd come back in the fall and take half of the increase in yield as his payment."

The hybrid corn performed so well that half of the increase in yield was worth much more than eight dollars, even in 1930, Garst said. "In the fall, Roswell would tell the farmer, 'Never mind, I won't hold you to that deal. Instead I'll take your eight dollars and your order for next year.'"

Roswell founded the Garst & Thomas Hybrid Corn Company in Coon Rapids. "By 1945, Midwest corn growers went from planting no hybrid seed corn to planting it on 100 percent of their acres," Garst said. This influenced a key developed that occurred during the height of the Cold War.

Roswell Garst, a plain-spoken, no-nonsense promoter of hybrid seed corn, urged Soviet premier Nikita Khrushchev to tour his Coon Rapids farm. Feeding the Soviet Union's people had become a huge challenge, and Khrushchev suggested that his nation needed an Iowa Corn Belt. It's hard to overstate the global impact of Khrushchev's visit to Iowa on September 23, 1959, a day that transfixed the world.

While Khrushchev failed to replicate America's ever-increasing agricultural production, his willingness to look to the West for ag technology left a legacy that hasn't been forgotten. "Khrushchev's visit to Iowa had a major impact on feeding the world," said Michael Michener, a New London, Iowa native and former administrator of the U.S. Foreign Agricultural Service. "We need partnerships like this today."

MR. WALLACE GOES TO WASHINGTON

Back in 1933, just as Henry A. Wallace's hybrid seed company was becoming established in Iowa, he was called to Washington to join Franklin D. Roosevelt's cabinet as U.S. secretary of agriculture. Wallace became one of the most important planners and administrators of New Deal programs.

"He proved to be a remarkable administrator of the U.S. Department of Agriculture, achieving a list of impressive accomplishments during the darkest years of the Depression, including price supports and production adjustment, crop insurance, disaster relief, soil conservation, surplus storage,

As the secretary of the U.S. Department of Agriculture, Henry A. Wallace endorsed the Agricultural Adjustment Act of 1937 when he appeared before the House Agricultural Committee. *Courtesy of Library of Congress.*

rural electrification, farm credit, food stamps and the resettlement of small farmers," according to the Wallace Centers of Iowa.

When he served as U.S. vice president from 1941 to 1945, Wallace became a world leader and popular author whose motto was "Peace, Prosperity, and Equality." He was a controversial advocate of international relations and humanitarian aid provided through the United Nations, especially for improved food production.

Wallace believed so strongly in the importance of world peace and cooperation that he became a candidate for the presidency on the Progressive Party ticket in 1948. The platform called for national health insurance, a guaranteed minimum wage, monopoly control, equal employment opportunities for women and equal pay for equal work.

After his defeat, Wallace retired from public life to his Farvue Farm in New York State with his wife, Ilo, to pursue his lifelong interest in genetics, breeding chickens, corn, strawberries and gladiolas. Wallace also worked to improve food production in developing countries. He had seen hunger and poverty during his travels and continued to work to promote increased production of food and provision of basic services.

After developing Lou Gehrig's disease, Henry A. Wallace died at age seventy-seven in Danbury, Connecticut, in 1965. His ashes were interred at Glendale Cemetery in Des Moines.

Perhaps Henry A. Wallace's legacy is best summed up by his quote shared by the Wallace Centers of Iowa. "If I were to draw conclusions from life, I would say that the purpose of existence here on earth is to improve the quality and abundance of joyous living."

John Froelich Invents the First Tractor in Iowa

Today, it's hard to imagine a cornfield without a tractor in the picture. Back in 1892, in the tiny village of Froelich in Clayton County, Iowa, however, folks were amused by what a local businessman, John Froelich, was saying. This northeast Iowa entrepreneur (1849–1933) believed that mechanical power had a great future—that someday traction engines would do the work of horses even on midsized and large farms. The locals had to admit, though, that Froelich had invented several handy gadgets, including a more efficient washing machine, plus he was a good businessman.

Froelich ran a grain elevator and a well-digging business and operated a threshing rig. Every year, he took a crew of men to Langford, South Dakota, to work the fields. Froelich had considerable experience with steam engines and knew their pitfalls: they were heavy and bulky, they were hard to maneuver and they were always threatening to set fire to the grain and stubble fields. On the flat prairie, with a strong wind blowing, that was no joke.

A frustrated Froelich decided he could invent a better way to power the engine. The solution was gasoline. Froelich and local blacksmith Will Mann came up a vertical, one-cylinder engine mounted on the running gear of a steam traction engine—a hybrid of their own making. They designed many new parts to make it all fit together, but finally they completed it. The word *tractor* wasn't used in those days, but that's what Froelich invented.

A few weeks later, Froelich and his crew started for the broad fields of South Dakota with the "tractor" and a new threshing machine. That fall, they threshed seventy-two thousand bushels of small grains. It was a success!

Later that fall, Froelich shipped his tractor to Waterloo, Iowa, to show some businessmen. Immediately, the men formed a company to manufacture the "Froelich Tractor." They named the company the Waterloo Gasoline Traction Engine Company and made Froelich the president.

Unfortunately, efforts to sell the practical, gasoline-powered tractor failed. Two were sold and promptly returned. The company then decided to manufacture stationary gas engines to provide income while tractor experiments continued, according to the Froelich Museum.

In 1895, the Waterloo Gasoline Engine Company was incorporated, but Froelich, who was more interested in tractors than stationary engines, chose to withdraw from the company. The Waterloo Gasoline Engine Company continued to build stationary engines while trying to improve the tractor. In 1913, the model L-A was made.

In 1914, the first Waterloo Boy tractor, the Model R single-speed tractor, was introduced. Farmers liked it, and sales reached 118 within a year. When the Model N Waterloo Boy with two forward speeds was introduced, it was also successful.

Northeast Iowa entrepreneur John Froelich (1849–1933) believed that someday traction engines would do the work of horses. In 1892, he invented the first successful gasoline-powered engine that could be driven backward and forward. *Author's collection.*

When World War I led to rising farm prices and strong demand for dependable mechanical farm power, the concept of the tractor became so popular that many tractor manufacturers sprang up in a matter of months. Deere and Company in Moline, Illinois, which manufactured a full line of John Deere implements, had been watching the progress of the Waterloo Engine Company and the increasing quality of its products.

Deere was looking for an established farm tractor to round out its farm equipment line, and the Waterloo Engine Company fit the bill. Today, Deere's facility in Waterloo remains one of the largest tractor-producing plants in the nation.

Charles City, Iowa, is also well known for the role it played in the history of the American tractor. The term *tractor* was first coined upon the unveiling of the Hart-Parr gasoline-powered traction engine—the first production-model tractor in the United States, according to the City of Charles City's website.

"In the winter of 1901, Charles Hart and Charles Parr came to Charles City, the county seat of Floyd County," noted the article "Iowa All Over: Charles City Is the Birthplace of the Farm Tractor Industry," which the *Cedar Rapids Gazette* ran on November 15, 2015. "While Hart and Parr were there, the two men built the first factory in the world to manufacture tractors."

From then on, tractors were built in Charles City for almost one hundred years. The growing business eventually became the Oliver Farm Equipment Company and finally the White Farm–New Idea Equipment Company according to the City of Charles City's website. At its peak in the mid-1970s, the sprawling plant complex encompassed twenty-three acres and employed nearly three thousand workers in Charles City. The 1980s farm crisis and other economic pressures led to the closing of the plant in 1993. Today, the Floyd County Historical Museum in Charles City preserves the plant's history through an extensive collection of documents, photos and artifacts, including tractors.

Carroll in west-central Iowa was also home to a tractor manufacturing company in the early twentieth century. In 1903, brothers Henry and John Heider started the Heider Manufacturing Company in Albert Lea, Minnesota. They moved the business to Carroll in 1904, incorporated the business in 1905 and began producing a four-cylinder, two-ton, all-purpose tractor in 1908.

As the Heider tractor plant evolved, it began producing the Model C "one-man" tractor. The 1915 Heider Model C cost $995 (about $25,000 today), according to the Carroll County Historical Society.

An early Heider brochure stated, "The modern farmer cannot afford to cultivate $150 to $200 land in the old-fashioned ways and with old-fashioned implements. Land is too valuable now to permit inefficiency in cultivation. He must use the latest-improved, high-efficiency farm machinery if he is to be really successful as a farmer. Every device that enables him to increase the yield of his fields or to produce his crops at least expense is essential to his success."

Another western Iowa company that brought new innovations to the tractor market in the early twentieth century was the Thieman Harvester Company in Albert City. The company manufactured Thieman tractors from 1936 to approximately 1942, according to *Farm Collector* magazine. The tractor originally came in pieces as a kit, to be assembled by the buyer, who had to provide an engine, driveshaft and rear axle.

The Albert City company was organized in 1921 by brothers Henry D., William B., Herman, Charles and Warren Thieman to make silage harvesters. (Silage is made from corn plants that are chopped and fermented to preserve the forage and provide nutritious feed for cattle.) Eventually, they produced livestock feeders and waterers, end gates, plow guides and saw frames, as well as steel burial vaults.

Beginning in 1936, Thieman tractors were offered in varied types: $185 kits, or a complete tractor with a Ford Model A engine for about $500. Those low prices were a welcome relief during the Great Depression. With the kit, the farmer had to procure his own engine, driveshaft and rear end from a Ford Model A or 1928 Chevrolet and then build a tractor. The object was to cobble together pieces of used equipment to make an inexpensive tractor.

A company brochure recommended a Model A motor "with new or reconditioned block, Model A Ford HD truck radiator, four-blade fan." The brochure also noted that full instructions for assembling were included.

"In his *Encyclopedia of American Farm Tractors*, C.H. Wendel notes that sales of Thieman tractors and kits were so brisk that as many as 150 people were employed 24 hours a day during peak seasons," *Farm Collector* reported. The need for steel for essential World War II uses ended company operations, however, in the 1940s.

While the era of Thieman tractors is long gone, these classic tractors are sometimes displayed at the annual Albert City Threshermen & Collectors show in August and the Clay County Fair in Spencer in September.

Hagie Produces Homegrown Ag Solutions

While tractors accelerated mechanical horsepower in farming, other innovations also drove the mechanization of agriculture. Sometimes these advancements emerged in a roundabout way.

Ray Hagie never intended to produce the world's first self-propelled sprayer. The Clarion-area farmer wanted to grow hybrid corn. In fact, his first piece of equipment—a self-propelled personnel carrier for detasseling corn—was built for his own seed corn fields.

But as Hagie Hybrids continued to grow, so did demand for his "above the crop" equipment. Hagie's Iowa farm became the birthplace of Hagie Manufacturing Company, as well as the world's first self-propelled sprayer, in 1947.

Three generations and millions of acres later, Hagie Manufacturing continues to provide some of the most advanced application equipment in the industry to help protect crops from weeds and diseases and to apply nutrients that help nourish plants. Hagie Manufacturing remains a pioneer in the ag industry with innovations such as front-mounted sprayer booms, hydrostatic drives, hydraulically adjustable booms and quick-attach systems that allow users to switch from a sprayer boom to a detasseler bar or a nitrogen toolbar in a matter of minutes.

Precision is the key with any application technology, said Newt Lingenfelter, product development manager at Hagie Manufacturing, during a 2014 interview. "Our equipment allows growers to take 8 ounces of a crop protection product—that's about the size of a coffee cup—and spread it evenly over an acre. When farmers can do this across their fields, it makes them more efficient and helps them become better stewards of the land."

Spirit of Service Drives Sukup Manufacturing

Innovation has also guided Sukup Manufacturing in Sheffield for decades. In the 1960s, progressive farmers were moving away from ear corn harvested by mechanical corn pickers stored in corncribs and switching to grain bins that held shelled corn harvested by a combine rather than a corn picker. (All these advancements made the labor-intensive job of picking corn by hand obsolete by the mid-twentieth century. In previous generations, an efficient farmer could harvest 110 to 115 bushels of corn per day by hand, while a few exceptional pickers could hit 125 to 130 bushels per day, noted Sac County farmer Arlin Sigmon.)

In the fall of 1962, Eugene Sukup, a young, innovative Iowa farmer, bought his first grain bin to dry and store shelled corn. He found drying to be slow, however, and pockets of grain began to overheat and spoil. To solve this problem, he modified a stoker auger from a coal furnace and inserted it in an electric drill. Then, using a chain, he hung it from the top of the bin to loosen the hot spots and prevent spoilage.

Sukup began making these stirring augers at a welding shop located nearby in Sheffield in northern Iowa. He sold five units to a local bin dealer for twenty-nine dollars each, but when he went back to check on them, he found that only three had sold—and one of those had been returned. To make a successful product, it had to be automatic.

Sukup went back to the drawing board and came up with the idea of adding a horizontal auger through the handle of the drill. He patented the idea, and the Stirway stirring machine was born. Sukup and his wife, Mary, founded the Sukup Manufacturing Company in 1963.

Throughout the years, Sukup Manufacturing Company has continually grown and expanded its product offerings. Sukup Manufacturing has become the world's largest family-owned and operated grain storage, drying and handling equipment manufacturer. From its headquarters in Sheffield, the business includes 1 million square feet of office, manufacturing and warehouse space. The key to Sukup Manufacturing's success has been its innovative ideas that have resulted in more than eighty U.S. patents.

In 2018, the company employed more than six hundred people, making it one of the largest employers in north-central Iowa. Three generations of the family are now active in the business, which has become a leader in advanced manufacturing in Iowa, specializing in portable and tower grain dryers, grain bins, steel buildings and more. "We embrace the use of technology in agriculture," said Steve Sukup, president and chief executive officer.

One of Sukup Manufacturing's most unique products that has gained worldwide acclaim took root after a January 2010 earthquake devastated Haiti. "Our safety director, Brett Nelson, wondered if we could try adapting our grain bins into durable homes," Sukup said. "We said, 'Yes, let's see what's possible.'"

This led to the creation of the Safe T Home®. Measuring eighteen feet in diameter and made entirely of metal, Safe T Homes are resistant to termites and moisture. They are also virtually earthquake proof. Each home can sleep ten or more people and features a double-roofed system that displaces heat. Each home also includes a full-size, lockable steel door, two windows that can be locked from within and a water collection system.

Sukup Manufacturing Company in Sheffield has become the world's largest family-owned and operated grain storage, drying and handling equipment manufacturer. It also produces the Safe T Home® (shown here at the 2018 Farm Progress Show near Boone). They are virtually earthquake proof. *Author's collection.*

"We now have about 250 Safe T Homes in various countries, including Haiti, Uganda, Kenya and Peru," said Sukup, who noted that his family's company typically keeps 20 Safe T Homes in stock.

Safe T Homes have proven they can weather the storm. In 2016, Hurricane Matthew devastated Haiti with winds in excess of 145 miles per hour. All two hundred of the Safe T Homes prevailed with just minor damage. In contrast, the storm destroyed the vast majority of traditional homes in the area.

"Everyone in a Safe T Home came out safe," said Sukup, who noted that each Safe T Home costs approximately $7,000, has a life expectancy of seventy-five years and can be assembled on-site with simple hand tools that are included with the Safe T Home.

Kinze Manufacturing Helps Farmers Produce More from Every Acre

As the Safe T Home story shows, it's one thing to hear about a need— it's another to address this need in a creative way. Some Iowa innovators, like Jon Kinzenbaw from Victor, Iowa, focused on the need to increase the efficiency of farming to help farmers get more out of every acre.

In 1965, twenty-one-year-old Kinzenbaw opened his own welding shop with a small bank loan and twenty-five dollars in his pocket. Anyone who knew him could see he had a talent for fixing things. No one could have predicted, however, that his small welding business would one day turn into one of the largest, privately held agricultural equipment manufacturers in North America.

"A customer told Jon he wanted a bigger grain wagon," said Rhett Schildroth, Kinze Manufacturing's product manager, during a 2013 interview with me. Back then, a typical wagon held 150 to 200 bushels of grain. "Jon was going to build a 400-bushel wagon but kept going until he ran out of steel."

It became clear that Kinzenbaw's massive 475-bushel wagon could increase farmers' efficiency dramatically, Schildroth said. The breakthrough that truly propelled Kinze Manufacturing on its stunning growth curve, however, occurred in 1975. After hearing some of his farmer friends complain about the amount of time they wasted dismantling and loading their planters onto trailers, Kinzenbaw invented a rear-folding planter toolbar. It revolutionized planting overnight. "There is nothing more powerful than a better idea and a satisfied customer," Jon Kinzenbaw said. "The first rear-fold planter sold 20 more, and the next 20 sold another 80. That's the way it happens."

These contributions are showcased in eastern Iowa near Williamsburg in the Kinze Innovation Center, which is open to the public and debuted in early 2013 at Kinze Manufacturing's world headquarters. "We're proud to have Kinze right here in central Iowa," said Governor Kim Reynolds, who spoke at the Innovation Center's grand opening.

IOWA'S HOMEGROWN HERO: WORLD FOOD PRIZE HONORS NORMAN BORLAUG

Not every Iowa ag innovator focused on machines to revolutionize ag production. A century ago, a young farm boy named Norman Borlaug felt he was called to become a teacher. Had Borlaug become a science teacher, as he once planned, this Iowa native might have affected hundreds of students during his career. Instead, he became the genius behind the Green Revolution and saved more lives than any person who ever lived.

Norman Borlaug, who grew up on a Howard County farm near Cresco, developed a high-yielding, disease-resistant wheat that launched the Green Revolution in the mid-twentieth century and saved millions of people worldwide from starvation. Borlaug was awarded the Nobel Peace Prize in 1970. *Courtesy of the World Food Prize.*

"Norman Borlaug is a hero," said Kenneth Quinn, president emeritus of the Des Moines–based World Food Prize, which recognizes breakthrough achievements in the fight against hunger.

Borlaug's legacy is preserved in the World Food Prize headquarters' Hall of Laureates, which is housed in the renovated downtown Des Moines public library. The project has renewed interest in the work of a quiet and self-effacing yet determined farm boy who never forgot his rural Iowa roots.

"Norman Borlaug led the single-greatest period of food production in human history, and this remarkable building preserves his legacy in an awe-inspiring way," Quinn said.

Born in 1914, Borlaug grew up on Howard County farm near Cresco and was educated in a one-room country school. In 1944, after earning advanced academic degrees, Borlaug accepted an appointment as geneticist and plant pathologist with the new Cooperative Wheat Research and Production Program in Mexico. In his quest to improve wheat yields in some of the poorest parts of Mexico, Borlaug first tried conventional plant breeding techniques but faced many challenges, Quinn said. "He would come close to success, but there was always something wrong. The wheat needed better disease resistance, or sometimes the plants were so lush with grain that they would fall over."

The "eureka!" moment came when Borlaug began working with Norin 10, a semi-dwarf wheat cultivar developed in Japan after World War II. Its thicker, sturdier stalks prevented lodging, and Norin 10 also allowed Borlaug to develop a high-yielding, disease-resistant wheat.

In just a few short years, Borlaug's highly adaptable wheat allowed Mexico to move from being heavily dependent on wheat imports to being a wheat exporter. It also benefited people around the globe, averting a famine that many thought was inevitable in India and Pakistan as the countries' populations boomed during the 1960s and 1970s.

This Green Revolution earned Borlaug the Nobel Peace Prize in 1970. Borlaug continued to work well into his nineties on behalf of the world's starving people. By the time Borlaug passed away at age ninety-five in 2009, he had forever changed the course of history and played a pivotal role with the World Food Prize, which he wanted the world to view as the Nobel Prize for Agriculture. "It's so important to carry on Norman's legacy," Quinn said. "The World Food Prize continues to inspire great the achievements that are needed to feed a hungry world."

Chapter 11

LIVESTOCK PRODUCTION THRIVES IN IOWA

Iowa has long been known as a state particularly well suited to livestock production, thanks to ample grain supplies, fertile land and abundant water. Today, Iowa is a powerhouse of pork, egg, turkey and beef production, claiming the top spot in the nation in terms of pork and egg production. Iowa's livestock farmers use science-based production principles focused on animal well-being to supply safe, nutritious food to people across the nation and around the globe.

It wasn't always this way, however. Until the post–Civil War era, the improvement of domestic farm animals had been "one of the most important, and to a large extent, one of the most neglected branches of rural economy," wrote Leila Mae Bassett of Iowa State College in her 1933 thesis "Agricultural Experiments in Iowa during the Civil War Decade."

Farmers like Godfrey Lenocker did the best they could to raise livestock responsibly. "We were hauling out manure all day, and it was a disagreeable job," wrote Lenocker in his diary on October 7, 1870. Lenocker had moved to Madison County, Iowa, in 1869 from Illinois and bought 320 acres of virgin prairie near Dexter for two dollars per acre. For years, Lenocker kept a diary of daily life on the farm. That invaluable historical record is now in the care of Lenocker's great-great grandson Ted Lenocker, whose family still lives in Madison County.

Hogs were an essential feature on many Iowa farms. From the 1800s into the early 1900s, hogs that produced ample amounts of lard were prized. In years past, lard was used in almost every farm kitchen in Iowa. The by-

By 1920, Fred Hassler of Manning was known as a top swine breeder in Iowa, thanks to his award-winning Poland-China hogs. Lard breeds grew quickly on corn, and their meat had large amounts of fat in it. This was considered desirable for improved taste. *Courtesy of the Leet-Hassler Farmstead.*

product of rendered pork fat, lard was used in baking and cooking and even in candle making. It wasn't until the advent of vegetable oils and vegetable shortening that lard fell out of favor, although some cooks are starting to favor lard once again. Lard is not only incredibly versatile but also the secret ingredient in some cooks' flaky pie crusts and fried chicken recipes, adding a desirable texture and depth of flavor to food.

As the livestock industry grew in Iowa, so did local sale barns, which could be found in small towns across the state, as well as large operations like the Sioux City Stockyards. The Union Stock Yards Company in Sioux City was first organized on January 21, 1884, to buy, sell and ship livestock on commission, according to Siouxcityhistory.org. In 1887, that was changed to allow the company to own and operate packing plants. Then the real growth of the stockyards began.

From its earliest days, the stockyards created a strong identity for Sioux City, as many local people and immigrants found work in the packing plants that developed in the city. The "big three" packing plants—Cudahy, Armour and

Swift—established themselves in the stockyards area by the late 1800s and early 1900s. (The meatpacking industry wasn't limited to Sioux City, since it also thrived in Ottumwa, Dubuque, Storm Lake, Denison, Perry and other Iowa communities at various times.)

Back in Sioux City, the many railroads in and out of the community aided the growth of the stockyards. Trains transported livestock (cattle, hogs and sheep) into town and fresh meat to market. Until 1923, nearly all of the livestock was delivered by rail. By 1953, however, nearly all livestock deliveries were done by truck, noted Siouxcityhistory.org.

The eighty acres of livestock pens, chutes and buildings at the stockyards hummed with activity for decades. Thousands worked in the packing plants and related businesses. Many a father would say to a child scowling at the aroma of the yards, "Smell that? That's the smell of money."

In 1973, Sioux City became home to the largest stockyards in the world, based on salable receipts, according to the *Sioux City Journal*. Everything changed by the early 2000s, however, in the wake of the 1980s farm crisis

Presidential candidate John F. Kennedy campaigned on September 22, 1960, at the Sioux City Stockyards. Sioux City became home to the largest stockyards in the world by 1973, based on salable receipts. *Courtesy of the Sioux City Public Museum.*

and massive structural changes transforming in Iowa agriculture, especially as small, independent livestock producers left the pork industry. The legendary Sioux City stockyards closed on April 1, 2002.

That doesn't mean livestock production faded away. With its assets of corn, soybeans, farmers and meatpacking capacity, Iowa still offers the ideal location for pork production, according to the Iowa Pork Producers Association (IPPA). "The 'Tall Corn State' also needs plenty of fertilizer to produce the bushels of corn and soybeans fed to pigs," added the IPPA. "Approximately 10 finishing pigs from weaning to market provide the nutrient needs of an acre of Iowa cropland on a semi-annual basis. Nutrients from one 2,400-head pig barn benefit a half-section of land (320 acres)."

The IPPA offers some other tidbits related to Iowa's pork industry, including:

- Iowa is not only the number one pork-producing state in America but also the leading state for pork exports.
- Iowa has more than 6,000 hog farms. Of these Iowa hog farms, 39 percent (2,451 farms) have one thousand pigs or fewer.
- At any one time, there are approximately 20 million pigs being raised in Iowa.
- Nearly one-third of the nation's hogs are raised in Iowa.
- Iowa producers market approximately 50 million hogs per year.
- 94 percent of Iowa's hog farms are family-owned enterprises.
- As of 2015, 141,813 jobs were associated with the Iowa pork industry. (That's roughly the combined populations of Ames, Ankeny and Coralville in 2015.)
- One in nearly twelve working Iowans has a job tied to the pork industry.
- Hog production contributed $13.1 billion to Iowa's economy in 2015.

Exports of pork from Iowa totaled more than $1.1 billion in 2017. Japan, Hong Kong, Canada, Mexico and South Korea are the leading customers for Iowa pork. While the United States was a net pork importer until the mid-1990s, America is now a major exporter, with more than 26 percent of U.S. pork being shipped to foreign counties.

Supporting the Iowa farmers who raise this pork remains the mission of the IPPA, which is based in Clive, Iowa. The IPPA, which was originally known as the Iowa Swine Growers Association, began holding meetings in the early

1930s to find solutions for disease control and improving pigs through better genetics, breeding and nutrition. By the early 1960s, pork production had evolved into an industry where more producers raised hogs only for market, while breeding stock producers became more specialized. Producers also began to recognize the growing number of factors that were affecting the profitability of Iowa swine operations.

A small group of producers was committed to promoting pork's message of a delicious, versatile product to reach more consumers. As the excitement caught on, county pork producer groups were formed, meetings were held and, in April 1968, producers formed the IPPA. Today, IPPA is a grass-roots organization that consists of approximately seventy county pork associations across the state, with more than four thousand affiliated and associate members. Every producer, regardless of size, has a voice in IPPA through a county-elected delegate system.

Part of IPPA's history has included an annual contest to select an Iowa Pork Queen and Iowa Pork Princess, who assist with pork promotions and educational activities statewide. The Iowa Pork Queen made headlines in 1991 due to a pie and an activist at the World Pork Expo.

Iowa has long been America's top pork-producing state. Ensuring animal well-being is important to pork producers like Erin Brenneman, who farms with her family near Washington, Iowa. *Courtesy of Erin Brenneman and Jen Madigan Photography.*

The annual World Pork Expo, which is held each June at the Iowa State Fairgrounds in Des Moines, is the largest pork industry–specific trade show in the world. It brings together nearly twenty thousand pork producers and other industry professionals from around the globe for three days of education and networking. In 1991, Iowa Pork Queen Dainna Jellings, nineteen, of Fayette had pie all over her face after being attacked by a woman dressed in a pig costume at the World Pork Expo. The pie-throwing woman was a member of People for the Ethical Treatment of Animals (PETA).

"It was a stupid stunt," said Vicky Eide of Ames, founder of the Iowa Alliance for Animals, who was quoted in an Associated Press article on June 6, 1991, titled "Pie 'Hit' Leaves Rights Movement with Egg on Face." "They have turned it away from being an issue for treatment of animals into an issue of treatment for humans by their blatant disregard for human dignity. They have demonstrated by this stunt they are more concerned about publicity and sucking money out of naive members than they are about animals."

FIVE REASONS WHY PIGS ARE GOOD FOR IOWA: A FARMER'S PERSPECTIVE

For decades, Iowa's pork producers have focused not only on animal well-being but, increasingly, on the environment. "We've always depended on a healthy environment to be successful," said Leon Sheets, a pork producer from Ionia, Iowa, who was named America's Pig Farmer of the Year in 2018. "We are better stewards of the environment than ever as we raise high-quality, nutritious pork."

A recent study from the University of Arkansas supports this. Producing one pound of pork in the United States has become much more efficient and environmentally friendly in the past fifty-five years, according to "A Retrospective Assessment of U.S. Pork Production: 1960 to 2015." During this time:

- 75.9 percent less land was needed to produce one pound of pork. This dramatic improvement was driven both by grain farmers raising corn and soybeans more efficiently and pigs converting that feed more efficiently. The improvement in land use is like reducing an eighteen-hole golf course to a four-hole golf course, according to the National Pork Board, which is based in Clive, Iowa.

- More than a quarter (25.1 percent) less water was needed. U.S. citizens would have to shower ninety fewer times a year to save that much water.
- 7 percent less energy was required. This energy savings equates to a typical household eliminating the use of a refrigerator altogether.

All these gains resulted in a 7.7 percent smaller carbon footprint for the U.S. pork industry. "The study confirms what we as producers have been doing to make good on our ongoing commitment of doing what's best for people, pigs and the planet, which is at the heart of the pork industry's We Care[SM] ethical principles," Sheets said.

Helping more people better understand modern livestock production is important to pork producers like Jason Folsom. He grew up on a crop and livestock farm in the Rockwell City area and has farmed full-time for nearly twenty years. Pigs have been an important part of his operation from the start. "Raising livestock was the only way I was going to get started in farming," said Folsom, who has five 2,400-head finishing barns on three sites and farms roughly two thousand acres with his father, Mike, who also has a 3,000-head finishing barn. "I like working with livestock."

Most of Folsom's swine barns are located near his farm home northeast of Rockwell City. "I always knew I wanted to farm and started thinking about it seriously in high school," said Folsom, who dabbled in construction work before farming full-time. "I like the independence of farming, watching things grow and being able to see rewards for your labor."

Producing high-quality pork starts with a focus on animal well-being. That includes providing proper nutrition, following tight biosecurity standards and maintaining a good working relationship with the veterinarian. "We focus on keeping the hogs healthy," Folsom said. "All this leads to a healthy, nutritious, affordable food source."

The hard work that's required to raise this food is just part of the job for pork producers like Folsom. If an ice storm or blizzard hits, Folsom heads to his hog barns to check on the livestock, often before he takes care of things at home. "Sometimes I don't think people realize how much the land and livestock mean to farmers," Folsom said. "Even though modern agriculture may look a little different than it has in the past, it's still family farming."

NORTHEAST IOWA FARMER
RAISES NIMAN RANCH PORK

Other Iowa pork producers like Chad Ingels raise pigs through Niman Ranch, a network that includes more than 720 independent farmers and ranchers across America.

Niman Ranch began in the early 1970s on an eleven-acre cattle ranch in a small coastal town just north of San Francisco. Niman Ranch producers raise animals outdoors or in deeply bedded pens. Niman Ranch livestock production protocols were developed with the help of animal welfare expert Dr. Temple Grandin and are some of the strictest in the industry. The company offers a complete line of Certified Humane® fresh beef, pork, lamb and a variety of smoked and uncured meats. "I've been with Niman Ranch since 2002," said Ingels of Randalia, Iowa, who runs a farrow-to-finish (birth-to-market) swine operation in northeast Iowa. "I like that Niman Ranch is focused on meat quality."

Ingels raises nearly sixty sows (mother hogs). About half are purebred Berkshire, which are known for intramuscular marbling that equates to exceptional flavor. The other half of the swine herd includes crossbred hogs with Chester White and Duroc genetics. Ingels's farm has been named among the Top 10 Niman Ranch farms in America for superior meat quality.

Ingels started raising hogs in 1991 after he graduated from Iowa State University (ISU) with a horticulture degree. While there were a lot of independent pork producers in Iowa at that time, the industry was changing dramatically. More farmers were opting to build large confinement barns, due to the reliable cash flow these systems could provide. The opportunity was attractive to both farmers and their financial lenders, Ingels noted. Confinement barns could also be built with the latest technology to make pork production more efficient.

This style of production works well for some farmers, Ingels said, but Niman Ranch suited his needs better. He could incorporate existing buildings on the farm and raise hogs in smaller groups. It's not always an easy livestock production system, though. "Weather can be extremely challenging for the pigs and me," said Ingels, a fourth-generation farmer. "Pigs grow slower in the cold of winter and the heat of summer. Since my barns aren't climate-controlled, the pigs eat a lot more feed in the winter."

Brutal winter weather can also cause gates and waterers to freeze, added Ingels, who noted that his type of pork production system is also labor intensive. Straw bedding must be replenished when female hogs are farrowing (giving birth and raising young pigs), while cornstalk bedding must be replenished in the finishing barn (where the older hogs live before going to market). "If there's a big snowstorm, it can take me a day or two just to move snow so I can access the bedding supply," he said.

Because sows and their piglets aren't confined in individual pens, there can be a risk to the babies. Mothers sometimes accidentally lie on their piglets and injure or kill them. "I've had a nice litter of ten pigs one day, and when I check on them the next morning, there are only seven piglets still living, because three were crushed," Ingels said.

Ingels feeds his hogs a mixture of corn, soybean meal and vitamins. Vaccinations are important to prevent diseases like pneumonia, circovirus and ileitis. Ingels raises antibiotic-free pork, meaning he doesn't administer antibiotics routinely. He can treat pigs with an antibiotic, however, if they are sick. "No matter how pigs are raised, whether in a confinement system or in a system like mine, withdrawal periods must be followed when using antibiotics," Ingels added. "That means no pork going to market can contain antibiotics."

It takes Ingels about six months to raise his hogs from piglets to 280-pound market hogs. Then the hogs are shipped to the Sioux-Preme Packing Company in Sioux Center in northwest Iowa, where they are harvested. "The pork I raise goes all over the country, from restaurants to grocery stores," Ingels said. He also sells some of his pork to local meat lockers, including the Edgewood Locker. "I really love hearing from people who enjoy the pork from my family's farm."

Ingels is not only a dedicated livestock producer but also a committed advocate for Iowa agriculture who is focused on improving Iowa's water quality. From 1999 until 2016, Ingels served as an Iowa State University Extension watershed specialist, where he worked with more than three hundred farmers on several farmer-led projects to enhance water quality in their area. Ingels has also served Iowa's Environmental Protection Commission, the governing body of the Iowa Department of Natural Resources (DNR). In 2018, he was a candidate for Iowa's secretary of agriculture.

Livestock production is good for Iowa, added Ingels, who has received various awards, including the Iowa Farm Environmental Leader award. "Livestock will always be my favorite part of farming. They keep you busy year-round, plus Dad always said, 'The pigs are the ones paying the mortgage.'"

CATTLE INDUSTRY THRIVES IN IOWA

Cattle, as well as hogs, have played an integral role in Iowa's agricultural history for decades. Iowa remains a top-ten cattle-producing state in America. The total cattle inventory in Iowa (as of January 1, 2019) was 3.95 million. In terms of all cattle and calves, Iowa ranks eighth in the nation, noted the Iowa Cattlemen's Association (ICA). Iowa ranks fourth nationwide in terms of cattle and calves on feed. In 2017, Iowa's cattle industry contributed more than $6.8 billion in business activity to Iowa's economy.

Many of these cattle producers belong to the ICA, which was formed in 1972. The group has nearly nine thousand members, including Iowa beef-producing families and associated companies dedicated to the future of Iowa's beef industry.

It's no bull that cattle are big business in Iowa, especially if you're around Audubon in southwest Iowa. While this small town boasts a picturesque main street, it's perhaps best known for Albert the Bull, the larger-than-life statue along Highway 71 that community members built more than fifty years ago.

Albert the Bull is the larger-than-life statue along Highway 71 in Audubon. An enterprising group of Junior Chamber of Commerce members dreamed up Albert in 1963 as a salute to the beef industry. *Author's collection.*

An enterprising group of Junior Chamber of Commerce members dreamed up Albert in 1963 as a salute to Audubon's beef industry. He attracts about twenty thousand people each year who want to say they've seen the world's largest bull statue. Today, the forty-five-ton, thirty-foot-tall Hereford statue isn't just a tourist attraction—he's a legend. When the fuel supply company Cenex was looking to showcase a rural community in a commercial for the biggest professional football game of the year, it featured Audubon and Albert the "Super Bull" during the Big Game in 2018.

In Praise of Cattle and Farm Dogs

In a world of uncertainty, one thing you can count on as a farmer is a loyal farm dog always at your side. More than companion pets, farm dogs play many roles, from providing a sense of security in remote rural areas to working with livestock. Many of the breeds of dogs that farmers rely on have a strong work ethic and thrive when they have tasks to do.

Just ask Laura Cunningham, who farms with her husband, Aaron, near Nora Springs. Their three-year-old blue heeler, Annie, helps move cattle and loves working every day on the family's northern Iowa farm. "There's less stress in the whole process of moving cattle when Annie's working with us," said Cunningham, who noted that blue heelers are also known as Australian cattle dogs. "Animals can communicate with each other. When Annie's working with the cows, they 'listen' to her and respect her."

Less stress for cows and people helps make farm work more productive and enjoyable for everyone. "Annie's great," added Cunningham, who grew up with black Labrador dogs on the farm. "She's smart, and her silly antics mean there's no shortage of laughs around here."

Dogs play a key role on many Iowa farms. Aaron and Laura Cunningham's blue heeler, Annie, rides in the tractor and also helps move cattle on the couple's farm near Nora Springs. *Courtesy of Laura Cunningham.*

After the Cunninghams adopted Annie when she was six months old, they began introducing her to the cows when she was nine months old. "She loves being outside and doesn't like to miss out on anything," Cunningham said.

When she's not helping to work cattle, Annie heads to the field. She enjoys riding in the tractor at corn and soybean planting time. She also likes to ride in the combine and the semi-truck at harvest.

Annie's work helps the Cunninghams raise high-quality beef for local families and restaurants. The family partners with Elma Locker & Grocery Inc., which is owned by a local family and specializes in harvesting and processing beef cattle, hogs and other livestock to provide farm-to-table, locally grown food. "Annie is an essential part of our farm," Cunningham said. "Not only does she work with us, but she brings the family back together at the end of the day."

RICK FRIDAY CARTOONS PUT AG IN PERSPECTIVE

Iowa's livestock producers aren't just hardworking entrepreneurs. They're also a creative bunch. Consider Rick Friday, a southern Iowa cattle producer and nationally known cartoonist. His farm-themed cartoons are featured each week in the regional newspaper *Farm News* and also appear in national publications including *Countryside* and *Backyard Poultry*.

"I try to convey a lot of thought in one picture," said Friday, fifty-nine, who raises cattle near Lorimor, Iowa. It's not unusual for cartoon ideas to pop into Friday's head when he's driving in the tractor. When inspiration hits, he often e-mails or texts himself the idea so he will remember it when it's time to draw.

This love of cartooning goes back to Friday's youth on the farm. At age four, he began drawing cartoon characters on his toy box. A few years later, he started drawing cartoons and selling them to the kids on the school bus for nickels and dimes. Sometimes Friday was scolded at school for doodling on his homework. "'He needs to focus more!' my teachers would say," said Friday, who was voted class clown by his peers.

Friday turned down an art scholarship in 1978. "I thought I would work and eventually farm," he said. While Friday did become a farmer near Lorimor, where his family had lived since 1890, his interest in drawing cartoons never subsided. "I think I'll always draw," said Friday, who credits his youth on the farm for teaching him a strong work ethic.

Rick Friday, a cattle producer from Lorimor, is a nationally known cartoonist. His farm-themed cartoons are featured each week in the regional newspaper *Farm News*. They also appear in national publications including *Countryside* and *Backyard Poultry*. *Courtesy of Rick Friday.*

Friday is inspired by Gary Larson, the famous cartoonist known for his syndicated cartoon series *The Far Side*. He still remembers the first time one of his cartoons was published in a newspaper in 1993. "I have my own character in my artwork," said Friday, who sometimes makes a rough sketch of a cartoon when he's working in the barn. "I also want to help save this rural life we have in Iowa. It's a beautiful, peaceful culture."

Helping the next generation of Iowa livestock producers thrive is important to Friday, a Union County supervisor who is helping a local young farmer get started in the cattle business. Friday's own cow-calf operation includes Angus/Hereford bloodlines that can be traced back to his grandfather's era.

Just as his farming operation connects the generations, so do Friday's rural-themed cartoons. "My goals are simple. I want to make people think and make people smile."

DAIRY EVOLVES INTO ROBOTIC MILKING, AGRITOURISM

Beef cattle aren't the only bovines that contribute to Iowa's livestock sector. The dairy industry has historically been important in Iowa and remains the fifth-largest sector of Iowa agriculture. In 2012, Iowa ranked twelfth nationally in total pounds of milk produced, according to *Iowa's Dairy Industry: An Economic Review*, published in 2012 by Iowa State University Extension.

Dairy operations of various sizes are located throughout the state, with the heaviest concentration of production in northwestern and northeastern Iowa. Dairy is good for business in Iowa. The economic impact of Iowa's $4.9 billion dairy industry includes 22,263 jobs, according to Iowa State University.

In years past, many small Iowa towns had a local dairy or creamery to serve the community. While the total number of creameries and dairy farms in Iowa has declined through the years, milk production per cow and total milk production continue to rise.

Milk production in Iowa during June 2019 (June is Dairy Month, by the way) totaled 433 million pounds, according to the U.S. Department of Agriculture's *National Agricultural Statistics Service—Milk Production* report. The

A robotic milking machine (shown here) dubbed "Rita the robot" milks cows at the Bolin family's New Day Dairy near Clarksville. The fifth generation of the Bolin family continues to modernize the dairy farm. *Author's collection.*

average number of milk cows in Iowa during June 2019 was 217,000 head. Monthly production per cow averaged 1,995 pounds of milk.

Some of this milk goes to Anderson Erickson (AE) Dairy, which was founded in Des Moines in 1930 and prides itself on "ridiculously delicious" dairy foods. AE remains one of the few family-owned dairies in America.

Iowa-produced milk also goes to Le Mars to Wells Enterprises Inc., which produces 150 million gallons of ice cream each year, including the famous Blue Bunny brand. "Wells gets all of its fresh dairy from within seventy-five miles of our production facilities in Le Mars," said Shannon Rodenburg, marketing and tourism manager for the Wells Visitor Center and Ice Cream Parlor. "Wells collects and processes more than twenty tankers of milk each day, 365 days a year."

In 2018–19, Wells invested $3 million in upgrades to the Wells Visitors Center and Ice Cream Parlor in downtown Le Mars. The destination includes an interactive "farm to spoon" look at ice cream production, from the dairy farm to the grocery store. The ice cream parlor offers an expanded menu with more novelties, extreme shakes and desserts, including the Lemon Meringue Shake, Monster Peanut Butter Cup Sundae, Molten Chocolate Lava Shake and more.

"This is a one-of-a-kind experience," said Adam Baumgartner, vice-president of retail sales for Wells Enterprises Inc. "Beyond the Iowa State Fair, we want to make this the single-biggest tourist attraction in Iowa."

Eggs to Turkey

Chickens and turkeys are also a big part of the state's ag sector. Iowa is home to 54 million laying hens that produce almost 16 billion eggs per year, making Iowa the largest egg-producing state in the country. "About one in every six eggs consumed in the United States comes from Iowa," said Kevin Stiles, executive director of the Iowa Poultry Association (IPA) in Urbandale.

For years, poultry production involved smaller flocks on nearly every farm in Iowa. A number of Iowa poultry businesses have served poultry producers in Iowa and beyond for generations, including the Murray McMurray Hatchery in Webster City, which mailed customers its first catalogue in 1919, and the Welp Hatchery of Bancroft, which has been in business since 1929. (To this day, customers can buy day-old young chicks shipped via the U.S. Postal Service.)

The IPA was formed in 1929 so poultry farmers could come together to discuss disease prevention and management tips and share best practices. Today, the IPA represents a broad cross-section of Iowa's poultry producers.

The impact of Iowa's poultry industry continues to grow. In June 2019, Iowa-based Hy-Line International Inc., the world leader in layer poultry genetics, opened the Dr. Henry A. Wallace Farm near Dallas Center. This state-of-the-art facility is increasing the population of research birds from which scientists can identify the top performing birds to populate the next generation of egg layers. Hy-Line supplies 40 percent of the world's poultry genetics and serves more than 120 countries, according to the company.

Turkeys are also big business in Iowa. Iowa ranks seventh in U.S. turkey production, with approximately 12 million birds raised annually, according to the Iowa Turkey Federation. Much of this turkey is processed into deli slices for sandwiches sold at Subway sandwich shops. "Subway makes enough sandwiches each year to wrap around the world six times," said Laurie Johns, former public-relations manager for the Iowa Farm Bureau Federation. "One of their most popular is the turkey sub, and that turkey meat is grown on family farms right here in Iowa."

The official "pardoning" of White House turkeys at Thanksgiving is a unique tradition that has captured the public's imagination for generations. In 1988, President Ronald Reagan participated in this event, which included Pete Hermanson (*to the right of the turkey*) and his wife, Janet, who were turkey producers from Story City, Iowa. *Courtesy of Iowa Turkey Federation.*

Sometimes Iowa turkeys make headlines for *not* ending up on the dinner plate. For decades, the president of the United States has received a turkey from the National Turkey Federation during Thanksgiving week. As part of the White House event, recent custom has the president "pardoning" the turkey, after noting the significance of a time of thanks for the nation's many blessings and the opening of the holiday season.

The first presentation of a turkey by the National Turkey Federation occurred during President Truman's administration. Since then, Iowa has supplied seven of the Thanksgiving turkeys pardoned by various presidents. Prior presidential turkeys have hailed from Ellsworth, West Liberty, Dike and Story City. The birds have represented Iowa during the administrations of President Johnson (1964), President Ford (1976), President Reagan (1983 and 1988), President George Herbert Walker Bush (1991), President George W. Bush (2008) and President Obama in 2016.

In 2016, the presidential turkeys came from Chris and Nicole Domino's farm nearly Early in northwest Iowa. "We were honored that the national Thanksgiving turkeys hailed from Iowa," said Gretta Irwin, executive director of the Iowa Turkey Federation. "Turkeys are a symbol of plenty and are a great celebration of Iowa agriculture."

"Peacemaker Pig" Floyd of Rosedale Helped Calm Racial Tensions

Thanksgiving turkey isn't the only livestock-inspired tradition that brings Iowans—and Americans—together. If you follow college football in the Midwest, especially if you're a University of Iowa Hawkeye football fan, you may know the story of Floyd of Rosedale. A bronze statue of the pig, Floyd of Rosedale, is exchanged between the two states. The original pig himself came from Rosedale Farms at Fort Dodge in north-central Iowa.

The whole deal emerged from a bet between Iowa governor Clyde Herring and Minnesota governor Floyd Olson about the outcome of the 1935 Iowa-Minnesota football game, but this story involves something much deeper than a famous pig and a bronze trophy.

The problem started the previous year, on Saturday, October 27, 1934, when rough play was directed toward one Iowa Hawkeye running back, Ozzie Simmons. Simmons was a rarity in that era: a black player on a major college football team. Dubbed the "Ebony Eel" by some sportswriters of the era, Simmons had come north to play football when he wasn't allowed to play football in his home state of Texas due to his race.

America in the 1930s included Jim Crow laws in southern states, which segregated black from white. In northern states, no such laws existed, but discrimination was still widespread.

Simmons's talent couldn't be denied, however, and he attracted the attention of a young Iowa sports broadcaster perched high above the field. That broadcaster, who would become President Ronald Reagan, became an Ozzie Simmons fan, noted Minnesota Public Radio (MPR), which aired the story "The Origin of Floyd of Rosedale" in 2005.

In the 1934 Iowa-Minnesota game, Simmons was knocked out three times, leaving the game for good by halftime. The Minnesota Golden Gophers overwhelmed Simmons and the rest of the Iowa team, beating them, 48–12. Iowa fans were outraged by how Minnesota played. They claimed that the defense deliberately went after Simmons hard. (Just eleven years earlier, Iowa State's first black athlete, Jack Trice, died of injuries sustained in a game at Minnesota in 1923.)

In 1935, the Floyd of Rosedale Trophy debuted in an attempt to generate some goodwill between the two schools. Olson sent a telegram to Herring to assure him the Minnesota team would tackle clean. To help calm the growing tension ahead of the Minnesota-Iowa football game, Olson said he would bet a prize pig from Minnesota against a prize pig from Iowa that Minnesota would win the big game. The loser would have to deliver the pig in person.

Word of the bet reached Iowa City as the crowd gathered at the stadium. Things calmed down, and the game proceeded without incident. Minnesota won, 13-7. The prize pig from Iowa was a Hampshire boar (a male hog with

The Floyd of Rosedale trophy is presented each year to the winner of the Minnesota-Iowa football game. This bronze pig had its origins in a 1934 football game marred by racial overtones. *Author's collection.*

black hair and a "belt" of white hair). The hog was later named Floyd of Rosedale after Minnesota's governor and the Iowa farm where the animal was raised. In the week following the big game, Herring delivered the live pig to the Minnesota Capitol building in St. Paul and took Floyd inside to meet Olson. Floyd the hog spent his remaining days on a farm in southeast Minnesota.

"When Ozzie Simmons stepped onto the field in October 1934 to play Minnesota, he entered a national drama that's still playing out today," MPR noted. "All Simmons wanted was a chance. The trophy is an ever-present reminder of how precious that right is."

Chapter 12

CROP PRODUCTION AND IOWA'S
EVER-CHANGING WEATHER

The livestock industry has thrived in Iowa for generations due to two key factors that allow farmers to grow bountiful crops that help feed livestock and provide an array of other benefits. Iowa's soil and climate make the state a prime location for the production of corn, soybeans, hay and other crops, plus Iowa has the infrastructure in place to support these industries. Iowa has long been the "Tall Corn State." The 1900 Census of Agriculture noted that Iowa led the Corn Belt in top corn yields, at 39.1 bushels per acre. Today, Iowa leads the nation in corn production. In an average year, Iowa produces more corn than most countries, notes the Iowa Corn Growers Association (ICGA).

In 2019, the state's farmers produced approximately 2.58 billion bushels of corn on 13.1 million acres, according to statistics from the USDA. Iowa's corn yield was estimated at 198 bushels per acre in 2019. Iowa has led the nation in corn production for the last twenty-six consecutive years and forty-one of the last forty-two years, USDA added.

Here are some other fun facts about corn from the ICGA:

- 99 percent of corn grown in Iowa is field corn—not the delicious sweet corn you might enjoy on the cob or in a can.
- While a small portion of field corn is processed for use as corn cereal, corn starch, corn oil and corn syrup for human consumption, it's primarily used for livestock feed, ethanol fuel production and manufactured goods.

Iowa leads the nation in corn production. In an average year, Iowa produces more corn than most countries, according to the Iowa Corn Growers Association (ICGA). This photo shows corn harvest on the Dougherty Century Farm between Lake City and Yetter. *Author's collection.*

- Corn is in more than four thousand everyday items, including shampoo, toothpaste, chewing gum, marshmallows, crayons and paper.
- One bushel of corn produces 2.8 gallons of ethanol fuel.

Nearly half a billion bushels of corn (461 million bushels), or 21 percent of Iowa corn, went directly into livestock feed in the 2014–15 marketing year. In livestock feeding, 1 bushel of corn converts to about 8 pounds of beef, 15.6 pounds of pork or 21.6 pounds of chicken.

Many farmers deliver corn to the local grain elevator, where the grain is either stored for a time, loaded on a semi-truck for delivery to local end users such as ethanol plants or feed mills, or shipped by rail, either to buyers across the country or to river terminals along the Mississippi River, where the grain is loaded onto barges and delivered to ports for shipment around the world. While some of Iowa's grain elevators are private businesses, many were established decades ago as farmer-owner cooperatives.

Although they are often defined by towering grain elevators, which have been called "the "skyscrapers of the prairie," cooperatives are so much more. Their unique business structure is based on key cooperative principles, including:

- OPEN AND VOLUNTARY MEMBERSHIP. Membership in a cooperative is open to all persons who can use its services and stand willing to accept the responsibilities of membership, regardless of race, religion, gender or economic circumstances.
- DEMOCRATIC MEMBER CONTROL. Cooperatives are controlled by their members, who help set policies and make decisions for the future of the business. Representatives are elected from among the membership to guide the cooperative and are accountable to the membership.
- CONCERN FOR COMMUNITY. Cooperatives are often the biggest employers in Iowa's small towns. Cooperatives grow the local economy and help support other local organizations, from volunteer fire departments to local schools.

Farmer-owned grain cooperatives provide a market for not only corn but also soybeans, which have been part of Iowa crop production for decades. USDA estimated Iowa soybean production at 502 million bushels in 2019, which were produced on 9.12 million acres of land. The Iowa soybean crop yielded 55 bushels per acre in 2019.

The Iowa Soybean Association (ISA), which marked its fifty-year anniversary at its 2014 symposium in Des Moines, has long focused on enhancing the long-term sustainability of Iowa soybean farmers. "We owe a lot to the soybean farmers who formed this organization and held the very first meeting in 1964 and to many others who helped build ISA over the years," said Tom Oswald, a former ISA president who farms near Cleghorn in northwest Iowa.

ISA, which is focused on expanding opportunities for Iowa soybean farmers, noted that:

- Iowa ranks second in the nation in soybean production.
- Nearly forty-two thousand Iowa farmers grow soybeans.
- Iowa farmers account for 14.5 percent of America's annual soybean production.
- The value of Iowa's soybean crop exceeds $5 billion.
- Every pig raised in Iowa consumes nearly three bushels of Iowa-grown soybeans, making pork production soybean farmers' number-one domestic customer.

Rail lines have long provided the vital infrastructure to link Iowa's grain-producing regions to the farm-to-fork network that spans the globe. This photo from the mid-1970s shows leaders of the West Bend Elevator Company by a rail car featuring the cooperative's name. *Courtesy of MaxYield Cooperative.*

Exports are also vitally important to Iowa soybean growers. Locks and dams on the Mississippi River that connect Iowa to ports in the Gulf of Mexico are essential to Iowa farmers.

Why are the locks and dams needed? The "Mighty Mississippi" is deep-flowing but turbulent in times of flooding; it's placid but shallow to the point of nonnavigability in times of drought. Other obstacles included swift and treacherous rapids, submerged rocks and boulders, uncharted sandbars and tree snags, which ended the lives of many riverboat steamers in the nineteenth century.

In 1930, after extensive studies by the U.S. Army Corps of Engineers, the U.S. Congress authorized the nine-foot channel navigation project on the Upper Mississippi River. This legislation provided for a navigation channel with a minimum nine-foot depth and a minimum width of four hundred feet, to be achieved by construction of a system of locks and dams, Construction of this "stairway of water" occurred from 1930 to 1940.

In the approximately 670 miles of river between the first lock at the Falls of St. Anthony area of Minneapolis–St. Paul, Minnesota, and the last lock of the project (Lock no. 27) at St. Louis, Missouri, the Mississippi has a fall of about 420 feet. The locks and dams create a series of "steps" that river tows and other boats either climb or descend as they travel upstream or downstream.

Many of the locks and dams on the Mississippi River are more than eighty years old but were only designed to last fifty years. Millions of tons of freight, including corn and soybeans destined for export, flow through the aging system each year via barges, noted a 2018 news report by Iowa Public Radio. Iowa ag leaders have been pushing for a number of years to get more federal funding to support infrastructure improvements to this vital farm-to-market link.

CORN VISIONARY AND THE IOWA HOG LIFT

Just as the locks and dams system helps connect Iowa agriculture to global markets, so do commodity groups like ISA and ICGA. This was evident during an ICGA gala dinner in December 2017 at the World Food Prize headquarters in Des Moines, when the name Walter Goeppinger came up frequently.

Born in 1911, Goeppinger was a lifelong resident of Boone, a 1933 Iowa State College graduate and a visionary leader for agriculture. Throughout his life, he was actively engaged in promoting U.S. ag products globally, making numerous trips to more than sixty countries on behalf of farmers.

In 1957, Goeppinger founded the National Corn Growers Association (NCGA) and served as its first president. Goeppinger's first major milestone on the international stage occurred in 1959 with the "Iowa Hog Lift." During the late summer of 1959, two huge typhoons hit Japan in less than a month, devastating much of Japan's Yamanashi Prefecture, an agricultural region northwest of Tokyo.

When Iowans heard about Yamanashi's plight, farmers from around the state donated hogs and shipped them by truck to Des Moines, where they were flown to Japan. Goeppinger became chairman and organizer of the Iowa Hog Lift under the volunteer People to People Program, which sent pigs and corn to Japan to help the country recover from the typhoons.

"At his own expense, Goeppinger made several trips to Washington, D.C., to negotiate with the Commodity Credit Corporation officers for a grant of eighty thousand bushels of government corn for the Yamanashi project," said Craig Floss, CEO of the ICGA. "During the next few years, the grain

During the late summer of 1959, two huge typhoons hit Japan, devastating much of Japan's Yamanashi Prefecture, an agricultural region northwest of Tokyo. Iowa farmers donated hogs that were flown to Japan. *Courtesy of Iowa Corn.*

handling structure in Japan was modernized to U.S. standards, and Japan's ability to feed its growing population significantly improved."

Within three years of the Iowa Hog Lift, more than 500 hogs had been produced from the original 35 hogs from Iowa. Within nine years, there were 500,000 hogs in Japan whose lineage could be traced to the Iowa Hog Lift.

In response to Iowans' generosity, the government of Yamanashi prefecture, represented by Governor Hisoshi Amano and his wife, traveled to Iowa and stayed with the Goeppinger family. In 1962, Japan's leaders expressed their gratitude by presenting to the people of Iowa a bronze temple bell cast with bold letters telling the story of the typhoon and Iowa's generosity in assisting the storm-ravaged prefecture. This "Bell of Peace and Friendship" is located in the formal garden of the state capitol in Des Moines.

"Not only did the Iowa Hog Lift evolve into the first sister state relationship of the People to People program, which is still going, but the Yamanashi Project was the forerunner of market development programs under USDA's Foreign Ag Service, which enable opportunities to trade U.S. ag products around the globe," Floss said.

Corn Palaces Once Reigned in Sioux City

While corn-fed Iowa hogs helped Japan more than sixty years ago, Iowa corn once provided the raw material to create larger-than-life architectural wonders in Sioux City. Magnificent corn palaces celebrated the agricultural bounty and economic power of the region in the late 1880s and early 1890s. "Like many other emerging middle western communities at that time, Sioux City was on the move," wrote the late Dorothy Schwieder, an Iowa historian who documented Sioux City's corn palaces in the spring 1973 issue of *The Annals of Iowa*.

The corn palace craze started in the summer of 1887. While a drought gripped much of the Midwest, the area around Sioux City appeared to be an oasis where abundant rainfall had produced excellent crops. This inspired local business boosters, who were eager to attract new people and enterprises to their community.

One idea sparked another, and soon people were talking about decorating a building with corn. "Then came the suggestion that marked the start of an enterprise never before undertaken anywhere in the world," Schwieder wrote. "Why not build a palace of corn?"

Sioux City architect W.E. Loft turned the community's corn palace dreams into reality. While his original design called for a fifty-eight-square-foot building to be located at the northwest corner of Fifth and Jackson Streets, those plans were revised to accommodate a one-hundred-square-foot temporary structure.

Finance committees were appointed to raise $25,000 (that's nearly $680,000 in today's dollars), and construction of the "Eighth Wonder of the World" was underway by September 1887. The project grew in scope until the completed structure contained 18,500 square feet of floor space.

Architecturally, the first corn palace defied classification, although it had many features of Moorish design, complete with a one-hundred-foot tower adorned with a huge cupola, arched windows, minarets and pinnacles. The windows were framed with ears of corn strung on wires, and the roof was thatched with stalks of grain.

Simple, natural materials became works of art inside the corn palace. A wax figure of Ceres, the goddess of grain, was adorned in a robe of cornhusks and held a scepter made of cornstalks as she stood at the top of a golden stairway made of corn. Murals made of grains and grasses on the interior walls depicted meadows, rivers, buffalo and more. Even the Iowa state seal was re-created from corn and cattails.

Between 1887 and 1891, the people of Sioux City built five corn palaces, each larger and more elaborate than the one preceding it the previous year. This picture shows the stunning 1890 corn palace. *Courtesy of the Sioux City Public Museum.*

While the corn palace officially closed on October 10, the following day President Grover Cleveland and his wife arrived by special train. "The president had taken a detour from Omaha to see the splendid castle of corn he had heard so much about," Schwieder wrote. "He appeared greatly impressed with the quality of the grain on display."

By the time it closed that year, the magnificent edifice had attracted more than 130,000 visitors. The corn palace also made headlines from the *New York Times* to the *London Times.* "Many of the eastern people were so favorably impressed with both the Corn Palace and economic future of Sioux City that the amount of eastern capital flowing into the city increased considerably," Schwieder said. "Sioux City citizens, jubilant over this success, decided to make the Corn Palace Festival an annual event."

Between 1887 and 1891, the people of Sioux City built a total of five corn palaces, each larger and more elaborate than the one preceding it. The second corn palace even featured "toilet rooms and conveniences for ladies and gentlemen," Schwieder said.

While corn palace promoters fully intended to create another in 1892, plans changed when a deadly flood ravaged the city in May 1892. Sioux City leaders felt they could not afford the added expense of a corn palace that fall, although they planned to bring the celebration back the next year. No one could have foreseen the financial panic that would soon sweep the country in 1893, Schwieder noted. Never again would Sioux City build another corn palace.

The corn palace craze of the late 1800s wasn't limited to corn. Iowans in the Creston area created bluegrass palaces to showcase the prosperity of the land and hard work of the farmers. In northern Iowa, flax (the raw material of linen cloth, as well as linseed oil) became the crop of choice for a palace in the 1890s. Local leaders built a flax palace in 1892 on the Winnebago County Fairgrounds in Forest City. The central block was three stories high, with an eight-sided wing on each side, noted Iowa Pathways, an online learning environment from Iowa PBS.

Weather Has Long Been the Talk of Iowa

When you're talking crops, it's a safe bet that the conversation will turn to the weather at some point if you're visiting with an Iowa farmer. As the old saying goes, if you don't like the weather, wait an hour. Sometimes, there's even a lot of truth to the adage that Iowa has all four seasons in one day.

Then there's the weather folklore that has endured from generation to generation. Before television, computers, weather radios and smartphones, people predicted the weather based on observation and tradition. It's hard to know if some of these nuggets of wisdom are fact or fiction.

"Lore that develops locally is 'right' more often than not, especially in the region where the saying originated," said Elwynn Taylor, an Iowa State University Extension climatologist who was quoted in the *Reader's Digest* article "The Scientific Basis for Popular Folklore that Predicts the Weather." "Folks who are greatly impacted by the weather, farmers in particular, pay heed to weather and any clues as to what is coming."

After I posed the question, "What weather folklore/weather sayings do you remember people talking about when you grew up in Iowa?" to the Facebook group "I Grew Up in Iowa!," more than four hundred people replied in a span of two days. Their replies included the following:

- Ninety days after heavy fog, there will be heavy moisture.
- The first firefly you see, eight more weeks of summer shall there be.
- When the snow sticks to the north side of the tree, it's supposed to be the last snow of the season.
- It's going to rain if the horse flies are biting.
- If the caterpillars have more fuzz, the winter is going to be colder.
- Rain on Easter Sunday, you will have seven Sundays of rain.
- It has to snow three times on a robin's wing before spring.
- Cows grouping tighter together, we're in for wet weather.
- When you see the first robin, spring is on its way. When you see the first red-winged blackbird, spring is here to stay.
- Red sky at night, sailors' delight; red sun in morning, sailors' warning. This is how you know if it's going to storm or not.
- First frost comes six weeks after the locusts start chirping.
- Plan on a snowstorm during the girls' high school state basketball tournament in March.
- When the leaves of the maple tree or most other flat-leaf trees flip over and you can see the lighter side of the leaf, it will rain within twenty-four hours.
- When the wind is from the east, it's not fit for man nor beast.

It's hard to forget the colorful weather-related expressions that tend to be heard on the farm, including "drier than a popcorn fart." At the other end of the spectrum are "frog strangler" or "million-dollar rain," if much-needed rain fell at the right time. While modern farmers rely on sophisticated weather apps and other technology to help track weather forecasts, measure rainfall and more, local weather lore lives on.

Although weather always has been and continues to be one of the biggest wild cards farmers must contend with, it's far from the only challenge in agriculture. An economic storm was brewing by the early 1980s that would forever transform Iowa agriculture and usher in an era that continues to reshape Iowa today.

Chapter 13

REMEMBERING THE 1980s FARM CRISIS

T
he hands that killed them are the hands that farmed the land, that fed the cattle, that raised the hogs. Weathered hands. Strong hands. Their own hands." So began "Anguish Forecloses on Lives of Three Farmers," which made front-page news in the Sunday *Des Moines Register* on October 13, 1985.

The sobering, heart-wrenching article continued. "Gordon Geiken, 45, drove a pickup truck down a dirt path near his Vinton farm, pointed a shotgun at his head, and died. Marvin Reed, 52, walked into the garage of his riverside Iowa Falls home, and he, too, turned a gun on himself. Steven Meeker, 32, went to an outbuilding on his Letts farm, strung rope around a beam, and laid a noose around his neck."

The three Iowa farmers all committed suicide in a single week—the seven days from September 20 to 26. None of them knew each other. "Their deaths are related only because they show that, as years of affluence yield to years of anguish, these are desperate times on the world's richest farmland," wrote reporter Blair Kamin.

As the farm crisis intensified, mental health experts were focusing on crisis prevention—trying to persuade desperate farmers from taking drastic action—including suicide. The article quoted Joan Blundall, consultation and education coordinator at the Northwest Mental Health Center in Spencer. "Folks just don't have the energy or fight to hang on any longer."

TRACING THE ROOTS OF THE 1980s FARM CRISIS

How did farmers in Iowa and beyond get to this point? Essentially, the agricultural boom years of the 1970s became the bust of the 1980s, as surplus production rose, too many farmers carried too much debt and interest rates soared to historic highs. As the number of farmers declined, the average farm grew larger.

In some ways, this trend could be traced as far back as the 1950s and 1960s. The rate at which young people left Iowa's farms for the towns and cities accelerated in the 1950s and 1960s. Data from the 1964 Census of Agriculture showed that there were 154,162 farms in Iowa in 1964, reflecting a drop of nearly 30 percent from the 214,928 farms in Iowa in 1930.

Future Farmers of America (now known as the National FFA Organization) has provided leadership opportunities for high school students in Iowa and beyond for generations. While many of these 1957–58 FFA members at Washington Township Consolidated School near Minburn envisioned a career in farming, that dream was shattered a generation later as the 1980s farm crisis intensified. *Courtesy of the Washington Township School Museum.*

The factors that unleashed the 1980s farm crisis were powerful and varied:

Many farmers took Earl Butz seriously when he told them to "get big or get out." Butz served as U.S. secretary of agriculture in the administrations of Presidents Richard Nixon and Gerald Ford. U.S. farmers increased production so much that there were record harvests between 1974 and 1979 in many areas.

Realized net income from farming in the United States averaged $26.8 billion from 1973 through 1975, compared to an average of $12.1 billion in the 1960s, according to grain embargo memorandums from 1976 in the Gerald R. Ford Presidential Library & Museum's online archives. Profitable production encouraged many farmers to expand.

Much of that expansion was financed with borrowed money. "It was the widespread substitution of credit for income during the past several years that is responsible for the current unfortunate plight of many financially troubled farmers," wrote Sue Ann Atkinson of Iowa State University in her 1999 thesis "The Farm Crisis of the 1980s in Iowa: Its Roots and Its Inner Workings." "Financial market conditions during the 1970s tended to encourage farms to use leverage in their growth strategies....As a result, it is not surprising that agricultural debt levels grew so rapidly during that period."

Expanding export markets for U.S farm products during the 1970s helped sell these extra bushels of grain, starting in 1972. Everything changed, however, after the Soviets, alarmed at the rise of militant Islamic political forces in Afghanistan, invaded Afghanistan in late December 1979. President Jimmy Carter was already under fire for what was perceived as a weak response when Islamic students in Iran had taken more than 50 American hostages at the U.S. Embassy in November 1979. On Jan. 4, 1979, Carter halted millions of tons of U.S. grain shipments into Russia. Presidential candidate Ronald Reagan denounced Carter's policy and vowed to end the embargo if elected.

President Reagan ended the embargo in April 1981. When his administration began working on the Farm Bill in 1981, Reagan attempted to set an overall limit on the amount of farm spending in the bill. Different farm organizations ended up fighting each other to get their piece of the pie. The administration also required that most farmers had to reduce their production acres by 10 percent to qualify for support payments. Farmers did what they had in the past—take their worst acres out of production and increase production on the rest, noted Wessels Living History Farm in Nebraska.

Inflation was running rampant through the U.S. economy in the 1970s. In 1979, the Federal Reserve Board tried to slow the rate of inflation by increasing interest rates. That increased the cost of doing business for all businesses, including farming.

Land is the first requirement for growing a crop, and land prices reached new highs in the production rush of the 1970s. From 1970 to 1981, when values peaked, national farmland values increased at an average annual rate of 13.4 percent, noted Atkinson. However, land that had sold for more than $2,000 an acre in 1980 dipped to the $700 range by 1986, she added.

When land prices crashed back down to earth in the 1980s, farmers who had borrowed money with escalating land prices as their collateral often couldn't get new loans, even for operating expenses.

"All of us who lived in Iowa at the time saw friends and neighbors lose their family farms and struggle with what to do next to earn a living," said Iowa Sen. Charles Grassley.

Ritchie Berkland knew exactly what he meant. The fourth-generation Palo Alto County, Iowa, farmer came of age as the go-go years of the 1970s gave way to the 1980s farm crisis. This marked one of the toughest periods on his family's Vernon Township farm, which had been in the family since 1891 when Berkland's great-grandfather, Christian Knudson, homesteaded the land.

After Berkland completed his degree from Iowa State University in 1975 and began farming full-time, he raised hogs and purebred sheep. Berkland and his wife, Cynthia, also began buying land, paying $2,995 for 80 acres in 1979. After the farm crisis hit, land prices plunged to less than $1,000 an acre in some areas.

To add to the pain, interest rates soared as high as 24 percent. "In those years, you couldn't make any money raising hogs, sheep, corn or soybeans," recalled Berkland, who moved his family into the basement of the farm home where his parents resided near Cylinder. "We lived there for thirteen and a half years, and we were glad to have my wife's income from teaching to help pay the bills."

Farm Crisis Intensifies

By 1982, the emerging economic crisis in rural Iowa spurred the formation of the Iowa Farm Unity Coalition, which would gain national attention through leaders like Dixon Terry, a farmer from Adair County in southwest Iowa.

Iowa newspapers also started reporting on the growing farm crisis. The September 30, 1982, issue of the *Iowa City Press-Citizen* ran the headline "Farm Crisis Day Planned Saturday."

"Declaring it's time 'to get some solutions hammered out,' a coalition of groups will hold a series of 'Farm Crisis Day' meetings in about 10 agricultural states from the Dakotas to Texas," the Associated Press article noted.

The Iowa meeting of the farm coalition was scheduled to begin at 10:30 a.m. on October 2, 1982, in Nevada, Iowa. Organizers hoped at least 300 people, including farmers, rural residents, labor organizations, church groups and business leaders, would turn out for the event.

The news out of rural Iowa only got worse as the early 1980s went on, even as the rest of the American economy thrived. By 1983, net farm income had dropped to its lowest level since 1971, according to data from the U.S. Department of Agriculture. Some farmers like Jim Dougherty, who raised corn, soybeans and hogs near Lake City, only made $800 for the whole year around this time. Other farmers reported negative income. Yet the darkest days of the farm crisis were still to come.

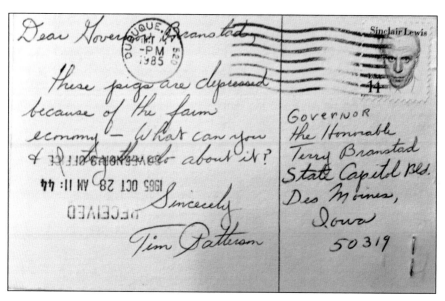

On the back of this postcard, which shows a sketch of two pigs on the front (with one shedding tears), Tim Patterson implores Iowa governor Terry Branstad, "These pigs are depressed because of the farm economy—What can you and I do about it?" The postcard was sent from Dubuque in October 1985. *Courtesy of State Historical Society of Iowa, Des Moines.*

"American agriculture is under its greatest financial stress since the Great Depression," stated economists cited in Atkinson's 1999 thesis. "Heavily leveraged farmers are having great trouble servicing their debts. Farm debt at the beginning of the 1970s was about three times annual farm income. By 1983 and 1984, farm sector debt was about eight times annual farm income."

On January 18, 1985, the article "Farm Crisis Rally Draw Thousands" made front-page news in the *Sioux City Journal*. Approximately four thousand people, including farmers, ranchers, bankers, small businessmen, clergy, elected government officials and others turned out for a three-hour event at the Sioux City Municipal Auditorium.

"The 1985 Farm Bill must give producers the opportunity to receive a fair price for what they produce," noted Tim Wrage of Emerson, Nebraska, chairman of the Farm Crisis Committee. "The decline of family farm numbers is affecting the entire segment of rural America through lost business, increased bankruptcy, high unemployment and increased psychological pressure."

The Farm Crisis Committee, which was started in November 1984 by eleven farmers and small-business professionals from Emerson, Nebraska, was said to have ten thousand members by late January 1985. The group received more coverage in the January 23, 1985 edition of the *Sioux City Journal*. According to the article "Without Help, Farmers See Sellouts," 43 percent of area farmers who attended the recent farm rally in Sioux City said they'd be forced to sell out within two years, unless economic conditions improved.

"A Tragedy of Awesome Proportions"

The January 23, 1985 edition of the *Sioux City Journal* warned "Economist Says Few Will Escape Spreading Rural Credit 'Cancer.'" "The level of emotional trauma…is a tragedy of awesome proportions," said Neil Harl, an Iowa State University economist. "It threatens to engulf the entire rural community. Few of us in the state will escape unscathed."

Tom Huston, Iowa's state banking superintendent, said 133 banks in Iowa had "more than normal problems." In addition, 48 Iowa banks were on a "problem list" at the Federal Deposit Insurance Corp., a federal agency that insured bank deposits up to $100,000 at that time.

Interestingly, the *Sioux City Journal*, had just run the story "Farmers' Poll Shows Satisfaction, Despair" on January 21, 1985. "Despite the difficult and serious financial problems facing agriculture today, Iowa's farmers are generally satisfied with their occupation. That's one of the findings from the fall Iowa Farm and Rural Life Poll conducted by Iowa State University," noted the article.

Close to half (41 percent) of the 1,585 farmers who responded to the poll said they were very satisfied with their occupation, while another 39 percent said they were somewhat satisfied. Just 16 percent indicated they were dissatisfied as farmers, and 4 percent were undecided.

Almost three fourths (72 percent) of respondents said they would be a farmer if they could choose their occupation again.

While 29 percent said they would recommend farming to a friend, 44 percent said they would not recommend farming, and 27 percent were undecided.

When asked whether they would continue farming if they had enough money to live comfortably, almost two thirds (62 percent) said they would continue farming.

Perhaps a poll respondent from Allamakee County in northeast Iowa summed it up best in his comment on the survey. "I myself enjoy farming, but it would be much better if there were some money in it."

Talk of a moratorium on farm foreclosures intensified. Iowa State University economists Neil Harl and Mike Boehlje told Iowa lawmakers there might be some benefits with the declaration of a foreclosure moratorium, but there would be a lot of drawbacks, too. Harl advocated debt restructuring.

"We would expect that if a moratorium were imposed, lenders would respond by raising the cost of loans to compensate for the higher risk, meaning the remaining borrowers would pay the price in higher interest rates," Boehlje added. The economists also noted that a moratorium would not forgive farmers' debts, guarantee their farm's survival or even halt farm foreclosures. All it would do would give some farmers a one-year reprieve once foreclosure proceedings had begun against them.

Farm Crisis Damaged More than Iowa's Farmers

When farmers experience financial problems, so do other businesses in rural areas. A 1985 report on the farm crisis, prepared for the Iowa legislature, anticipated a loss of 25 percent of the firms in the agribusiness sector, as Atkinson noted in her thesis. "For rural areas that do not have a lot of businesses because of the sparser population, losing 25 percent of their businesses can be devastating," she added.

The farm crisis soon spread far beyond Iowa's farms. It decimated small towns, where many businesses closed. It also hit Iowa's bigger cities hard, especially cities where farm implement manufacturers, meatpacking plants and other ag-related businesses were based.

Between 1980 and 1990, the eastern Iowa city of Dubuque lost 7.8 percent of its population, dropping to 57,500 in 1990. As double-digit unemployment persisted, many residents left both the city and the state, leaving many downtown businesses struggling. Property tax rates increased, while the average home value fell by 9 percent, noted the City of Dubuque's website.

As the downward trend continued, neighborhoods were left disconnected as 10 percent of the housing in Dubuque was vacant or available for sale. People grew desperate, and citizens had little hope that anything would change. In January 1982, as Dubuque's unemployment hit a record high of 23 percent, a billboard proclaimed, "Would the last person to leave Dubuque please turn off the lights?"

Dubuque wasn't the only Iowa city that was suffering. The Caterpillar Tractor Company plant in Burlington, Iowa, closed in 1984, noted Iowa PBS's documentary film *The Farm Crisis*. The Quad Cities in eastern Iowa and western Illinois lost an estimated twenty thousand manufacturing jobs during this time. As demand plummeted, John Deere, the largest farm implement manufacturer in the region, laid off workers by the thousands. Waterloo in northeast Iowa lost 14 percent of its population in the early 1980s, and scores of homes were left abandoned.

Fifteen Thousand Gathered at Hilton Coliseum

Tensions across Iowa continued to grow, as there was no relief in sight to the farm crisis. "I dreaded every time the phone rang back then," said Bill Bruggeman, a farmer from Carroll County who passed away in 2019. "You never knew who it might be or what bad news it might bring."

While the Iowa economy as a whole was suffering, things could soon get worse, stressed Iowa farmer Dixon Terry from Adair County and activist David Ostendorf in their *Des Moines Register* editorial "What the State Could Do to Help Alleviate the Farm-Debt Crisis."

"There is no longer a farm crisis or a rural crisis, but a crisis for all of Iowa and the nation," the pair wrote in the opinion page of the February 7, 1985 edition. "We will continue to see our soil- and water-resource base deteriorate as our family farm system collapses. And if the food-production system comes to resemble the energy industry, in terms of corporate control, then everyone who eats will pay the price for losing the family farmer. The situation has now reached the point where only immediate, bold and unified action will prevent the destructive shift toward that kind of future."

Maybe it was no wonder when more than fifteen thousand people jammed Hilton Coliseum in Ames on February 27, 1985, for the "National Crisis Action Rally" to protest "ruthless" federal farm policies and cheer speakers who said "this administration has declared war on the family farm."

"I come before you today to tell you that if we do nothing, the bells will have tolled the end of an American dream," Bishop Maurice Dingman of Des Moines's Roman Catholic Diocese told the rally, where some in the overflow crowd had to stand outside and listen to loudspeakers broadcasting the speeches being delivered inside Hilton Coliseum.

Speaker after speaker from groups like the National Farmers Organization, the National Grange and the National Farmers Union called for federal help, fundamental farm policy reform and cooperation among farmers, noted the Associated Press story "America's Farmers: Hard Times Turning Farmers into Activists," which appeared in newspapers across the country in early March 1985.

In Washington, D.C., a delegation of congressional Democrats led by Senator Tom Harkin of Iowa planted approximately 250 small white wooden crosses in Lafayette Park, across Pennsylvania Avenue from the White House, to dramatize their demand for the administration to help farmers.

AMERICA NEEDS FARMERS

Someone who heard the message loud and clear wasn't a politician, but a Big 10 football coach. Hayden Fry, head football coach at the University of Iowa, knew that the farm crisis touched many of his players and most of the fans. He was rebuilding the Hawkeye football legacy and wanted to show the nation that the strength of his team could also be measured in their character.

Hayden Fry, head coach the University of Iowa football team during the 1980s, supported the new America Needs Farmers (ANF) logo, which players still wear during games. It remains a testament to the men and women who provide the nation's food supply. *Courtesy of the University of Iowa.*

Never one to accept defeat, Fry quietly went to work on a game plan to raise awareness of farmers who were struggling. Fry himself was a former farm boy, raised with the values of hard work and integrity on his family's farm in Texas.

When Fry's squad traveled to Ohio State on November 2, 1985, something new appeared on their game-day helmets: a simple yellow circle, two and a half inches wide, with the letters "A-N-F" positioned immediately above the iconic Tigerhawk logo on the right side of the headgear. It stood for "America Needs Farmers." In that moment, and through the many games, players and wins that followed, the ANF logo remains a testament to the men and women who proudly give their all to provide the nation's diverse food supply.

Back in 1985, the Iowa Hawkeyes would go on to win the Big 10 championship and advance to the 1986 Rose Bowl. Fry, who received an honorary Iowa Farm Bureau Federation (IFBF) membership, said, "The thing I'm most proud of here at Iowa is putting the ANF on our headgear."

The ANF logo and spirit continue to live on each year through the University of Iowa and IFBF promotions that honor Iowa's farmers.

"Today, less than five percent of Iowans make a living from the land," noted IFBF. "There may be fewer Iowa farmers, but they are more diversified, innovative and efficient, and have weathered new challenges to the way they grow our food and energy. Their job to grow safe, wholesome food has never been more important."

A DEADLY ENDING TO 1985

While the ANF news from Iowa City offered hope in a time of despair, the Johnson County area would also witness one of the deadliest legacies of the farm crisis before 1985 ended.

When people across the country opened their morning newspaper on December 10, 1985, they were greeted by headlines of a murder-suicide in rural Iowa. "A farmer who was apparently distraught over his finances killed the president of his bank and is believed to have slain a neighbor and his own wife before he killed himself, the authorities said," stated the *New York Times'* article "4 Dead in Rampage in an Iowa Town."

Dale Burr, sixty-three, who farmed near Lone Tree, Iowa, a small town southeast of Iowa City, walked into the Hills Bank and Trust Company shortly before noon on December 9, 1985, where he shot and killed the bank president, John Hughes, with a twelve-gauge shotgun.

That same day, Burr also killed his wife, Emily, and a neighbor, Richard Goody. Burr was stopped by a deputy along a gravel road about a mile from his home. Burr killed himself in his truck while the deputy waited for other officers to arrive, noted a statement released at the time by the Johnson County Sheriff's Office. "Johnson County authorities said Burr's shooting spree apparently resulted from mounting debts and a dispute with Goody over farming 80 acres of land," according to United Press International story dated December 13, 1985.

"No one will ever know the complete truth about Dale Burr's rampage through this community of rolling hills and family farms in southeastern Iowa last December 9," wrote *Inc.* magazine in a 1986 article "On the Road: Johnson County, Iowa." "But the shotgun blasts he fired that day would startle the nation. America's farm crisis, it seemed, was turning bloody."

BETTER DAYS AHEAD

The Farm Crisis was far from over as the 1980s wore on, but times were changing. By 1987, the U.S. Congress passed the Agricultural Credit Act to provide and administer financial and technical assistance to weak financial institutions. Iowa's farm foreclosure moratorium remained in place. The moratorium allowed farmers to avoid foreclosure by making interest payments on land loans, even if they could not meet principal payments.

The February 2, 1988 edition of the *Sioux City Journal* carried the article "Farm Foreclosure Moratorium Sails through Senate." It noted that Governor Terry Branstad invoked the moratorium by declaring a state of economic emergency in October 1985. This was renewed annually by mutual agreement of the state legislature and governor.

One thing that was clear by 1988 was that a severe drought was gripping some parts of Iowa that summer, adding insult to injury for rural Iowans trying survive the farm crisis. Ritchie Berkland didn't even make one hundred bushels per acre of corn on his Palo Alto County farm that year. Despite the tough times, he and his family were able to keep farming. Within a few years, Berkland had begun selling seed to supplement the family's income.

The fact that the family survived the farm crisis was no small accomplishment, added Berkland, whose family received a Century Farm Award in 2011 for owning the same farmland for one hundred years or more. "A century farm is a connection to family, from my ancestors to my siblings to my children," he said. "This is a gathering place, and we're glad we've kept the farm in our family."

Not all farm families were as fortunate as the Berklands. Before the 1980s farm crisis hit, Iowa was home to 121,000 family farms. Nearly 20,000 failed during the 1980s, ending generations of farm legacy for many family farms. Nationally, the farm crisis claimed nearly 235,000 family farms, according to the Iowa Farm Bureau Federation's America Needs Farmers website. "Ultimately, a quarter of Iowa's farms would disappear during the 1980s," added Pamela Riney-Kehrberg, a history professor at Iowa State University.

Iowa farmers who survived the farm crisis of the 1980s and weather extremes of the late 1980s gained a more profound understanding of what their parents and grandparents had endured during the Great Depression. Roy Bardole, who farms near Rippey in Greene County, thinks of his father, Paul, who started farming in the early 1930s on land his ancestors bought in 1901. "He didn't talk much about those days, but he lived them the rest of his life," said Bardole, who began farming with his father full-time after earning his farm operations degree from Iowa State University in 1965.

Bardole himself would be forever changed by 1980s farm crisis. While he has continued to update his farming operation, even becoming the face of modern technology in a 2013 exhibit featuring American agriculture at the Smithsonian National Air and Space Museum in Washington, D.C., those farm crisis days are never forgotten. "The big lesson I learned during the 1980s? Be careful," said Bardole, who farms his family's Century Farms with his sons and grandson.

Chapter 14

CONSERVING IOWA'S NATURAL RESOURCES

One legacy of the turbulent 1980s is a renewed commitment to conservation. Perhaps the most visible result is the Conservation Reserve Program (CRP), which has been called one of the most successful private land conservation programs in American history.

Created through the 1985 Farm Bill, the CRP is a U.S. Department of Agriculture program designed to protect the environment. In exchange for rental payments, farmers remove environmentally sensitive land (such as highly erodible acres) from crop production and add plant species such as native grasses that help conserve and improve soil, protect water quality and provide wildlife habitat.

By 2017, more than 15 percent of America's agricultural land was in conservation programs like CRP, along with the Environmental Quality Incentives Program (EQIP) and Conservation Stewardship Program (CSP), noted Dr. John Newton, chief economist for the American Farm Bureau Federation. In Iowa, 12 percent of the state's farm acres were in conservation programs in 2017, added Newton, who spoke at the Ninety-Second Annual Soil Management Land Valuation Conference in Ames in the spring of 2019.

Conservation in Iowa goes back much farther than 1985, however. A move to protect natural resources was taking root in the 1930s, when young men with the federal government's Civilian Conservation Corps (CCC) worked on hundreds of Iowa farms. They assisted with a variety of soil erosion–control projects, including terracing hills, digging ponds, repairing gullies and planting trees for wind breaks.

RIDING WITH TRUMAN

Conservation in Iowa began gaining national attention decades ago, thanks to the National Plowing Match and Soil Conservation Day in Dallas County on September 18, 1948. President Harry Truman spoke at the event, where a huge crowd of 100,000 people gathered on Lois Agg's farm to see new conservation practices in action and hear Truman deliver a speech about farm policy.

After the speech, Truman and his entourage dined on fried chicken before heading out to the demonstration sites to see terraces, ponds and other conservation practices. Truman jumped off the hayrack to get a closer look, as members of the Secret Service scrambled to catch up with him.

"Truman was very interested in soil conservation and asked us a lot of questions," said Bob Larson, who was running some of the equipment at the conservation demonstration area. "While some guys thought terraces and contour farming were crazy, many farmers were intrigued by new conservation practices that were being promoted by the Soil Conservation Service."

After speaking at the National Plowing Match and Soil Conservation Day near Dexter to a crowd of 100,000 people on September 18, 1948, President Harry Truman greeted farmers before heading to the field to see terraces, ponds and other conservation practices. *Courtesy of the Dexter Museum.*

Truman took off his suit jacket, rolled up his sleeves on that hot afternoon and continued asking questions as he rode on Larson's bulldozer while the Secret Service looked on. Larson wasn't nervous as he chauffeured the president. "Truman was just an old farmer who wanted to know practical things, like how much dirt I was hauling."

Truman went on to win the presidential election in November 1948. Truman's appearance at Dexter also helped usher in the modern era of conservation in agriculture.

Aldo Leopold's Land Ethic

Truman isn't the only famous name with ties to Iowa and conservation. Aldo Leopold (1887–1948), a native of Burlington in southeastern Iowa, saw a need for wise use of land and water resources.

Even as a child, Leopold showed a keen interest in the natural world, noted the Biographical Dictionary of Iowa digital archive. At age eleven, he wrote a school composition on wrens in which he identified thirty-nine species he had observed. His father, who had a disciplined code of sportsmanship, taught him to hunt when Leopold was about twelve.

As a result, the internationally known conservationist, ecologist and educator devoted his life to planting the seeds of thought about how farming should be productive but not interfere with natural systems. An early graduate from Yale University's School of Forestry, Leopold worked many years for the U.S. Forest Service in the Arizona and New Mexico territories. He helped found the Wilderness Society and the Wildlife Society and was active in numerous conservation organizations.

During his sixty-one years, he published nearly five hundred works, including technical reports, speeches, textbooks, newsletters, reviews and even a few poems. But he is best known for *A Sand County Almanac*, a collection of forty-one essays published after his death in 1948. In this influential work, Leopold outlined his famous "land ethic" and development of an ecological conscience.

This grew from a lifetime of experience and careful observations of nature, including his experiences in rural Wisconsin. In 1935, Leopold purchased a run-down farm on the Wisconsin River near Baraboo and began a long-term ecological restoration project. His entire family contributed to the effort, rebuilding a chicken coop into a cabin, known as

Burlington native Aldo Leopold wrote *A Sand County Almanac*, which outlined his famous "land ethic" and development of an ecological conscience. *Courtesy of the Aldo Leopold Foundation.*

the Shack, and spending countless weekends planting trees and restoring prairie areas.

The farm gave Leopold time to observe and think about the complex relationships between land and humans. At its core, Leopold's idea of a land ethic is simply caring about people and land and strengthening the relationships between them, noted the Wisconsin-based Aldo Leopold Foundation. "When we see land as a community to which we belong, we may begin to use it with love and respect," Leopold wrote.

He believed that direct contact with the natural world was crucial in shaping our ability to extend our ethics beyond our own self-interest. He hoped that his essays would inspire others to embark or continue on a similar lifelong journey of outdoor exploration, developing an ethic of care that would grow out of their own close personal connection to nature.

Unfortunately, Leopold did not live to witness the full power of his ideas. He died in 1948 of a heart attack while helping to fight a wildfire that threatened the farm he loved. His legacy and his name live on in countless ways, however, including the Leopold Center for Sustainable Agriculture at Iowa State University. The Leopold Center was created in 1987 as part of the Iowa Groundwater Protection Act. The goals of the center have been to identify and develop new ways to farm profitably while conserving natural resources and reducing negative environmental and social impacts.

Don't Farm Naked, Grow Cover Crops

Today's Iowa farmers continue to incorporate more conservation practices, including cover crops, into their farming methods. Cover crops (including small grains like rye) create a living cover on the landscape when the cash crop of corn or soybeans isn't growing. Numerous studies have shown these plants can help protect soil and water quality, reduce chemical input costs, enhance soil health, improve farm resiliency, boost yields, increase forage availability and improve wildlife habitat.

In Iowa, the number of cover crop acres has increased dramatically in recent years, from fewer than 10,000 acres in 2009 to 880,000 acres in 2018. Practical Farmers of Iowa (PFI) has played a central role in bringing about this transformative change to the landscape. Leading the way is Sarah Carlson, who began working for PFI in 2007 while she earned her master's degree in crop production/physiology and sustainable agriculture from Iowa State University (ISU). "My philosophy? Don't farm naked; plant cover crops," Carlson said. "Think roots in the ground year-round."

Carlson, who received the 2018 Leadership in Conservation Award, has earned a reputation as a no-nonsense agronomist driven by a passion to revive rural communities, one farmer at a time. "My vision is to fill rural church pews and school buses by helping farmers diversify their operations while protecting and improving their soil."

Carlson is encouraged by the progress that's being made in Iowa and the Midwest to add more cover crops to help address water quality challenges. "Every day I see more crop and livestock farmers asking questions about cover crops for their operations. There's more work to be done, but we're moving in the right direction."

IMPROVING IOWA'S WATER QUALITY

Continual improvement is also reflected in rural Iowa as more farmers adopt new methods to protect water quality. When Tim Smith signed up for the Mississippi River Basin Healthy Watersheds Initiative in 2011, he wasn't worried about the required water testing that accompanied the conservation practices he was adopting on his Wright County fields. He was looking for ways to do more to protect water quality, including adding a bioreactor in his field to help keep excess nutrients known as nitrates out of nearby streams and rivers.

A bioreactor consists of a buried pit filled with a carbon source like wood chips where beneficial microbes live. The bioreactor is located at the edge of a farm field. Water that is drained from the soil through ag tiles in the field passes through the bioreactor, which acts like a "coffee filter" to reduce nitrates (thanks to help from the beneficial microbes) by an average of 43 percent, according to the Iowa Nutrient Reduction Strategy. Bioreactors offer a proven tool to help protect Iowa's water quality by keeping nutrients in the soil, where they can nourish crops, rather than letting them enter Iowa's waterways.

"I thought I was doing everything right with nitrogen management," said Smith, who raises four hundred acres of soybeans and four hundred acres of corn east of Eagle Grove. "The first year, though, my water samples showed that my nitrate levels were higher than the levels in the stream."

Nitrate levels from Smith's farm were in the 19 to 20 parts per million (ppm) range, while levels in the stream were 17 to 18 ppm. The U.S. Environmental Protection Agency (EPA) has set the primary drinking water standard (from public water supplies) for nitrate at 10 ppm.

Smith has worked with the water testing lab at the Iowa Soybean Association's (ISA) headquarters in Ankeny to monitor his nitrate levels. By periodically pulling samples over a period of several years, he was able to spot trends in the nitrate levels coming from his farm. Nitrate levels dropped as he adopted more conservation practices, including cover crops.

"By the third year after we started testing, nitrate levels in the water samples from my field were lower than the nitrate levels in the stream," said Smith, who has also worked with Natural Resources Conservation Service (NRCS) staff on water quality testing.

In fact, nitrate levels in the water leaving the bioreactor on Smith's farm dropped to 4 ppm, while nitrate levels from other testing sites on his farm dipped below 10 ppm. "This information was really eye opening," said Smith, who now seeds 525 acres of cereal rye on his land. "It's clear you have to be intentional about adopting new solutions to help improve water quality."

Prairie Strips to Pollinators

Prairie strips placed strategically within Iowa fields are also providing impressive results to help row-crop operations meet key environmental goals.

Iowa State University researchers, along with farmers, extension specialists and others, are exploring the potential of Science-based Trials of Rowcrops Integrated with Prairie Strips (STRIPS) as a conservation practice. STRIPS trials have been conducted at the Neal Smith National Wildlife Refuge in Jasper County since 2005 and are also being implemented in other parts of Iowa.

By converting 10 percent of a crop field to diverse, native perennials, farmers and farmland owners can reduce the amount of soil leaving their fields by 95 percent and the amount of nitrogen leaving their fields through surface runoff by up to 85 percent, according to ISU. Prairie strips also provide habitat for wildlife, including pollinators and other beneficial insects.

"Prairie is starting to gain respect as a conservation alternative with multiple potential advantages," noted Laura Jackson, professor of biology and director of the Tallgrass Prairie Center at the University of Northern Iowa. "These research projects are an important way to help landowners find answers they need so we can scale up this practice that is an important part of Iowa's unique heritage."

These solutions benefit pollinators such as monarch butterflies. "All of Iowa's acres fall within the prime range of the monarchs' breeding habitat," said Dana Schweitzer, program coordinator for the Iowa Monarch Conservation Consortium at Iowa State University.

Wayne Fredericks, a northern Iowa soybean and corn farmer from Osage, was inspired to add pollinator habitat to his land after learning about the monarchs' declining populations. "My philosophy is that monarch habitat and production agriculture can co-exist," said Fredericks, who participates in the Conservation Reserve Program and has partnered with the wildlife conservation group Pheasants Forever to develop a seed mix suited to his acres, including Black-Eyed Susans and other blooming plants.

Since 2014, Fredericks has added seven small pieces of pollinator habitat on his land, from a 3.2-acre plot near a pond to a pollinator plot that measures $7/10$ of an acre in a filter strip, which controls runoff from the field. "That's a win-win, since it benefits pollinator habitat and water quality," Fredericks said.

These habitat areas also attract other species of butterflies, deer, birds and wildlife. "In 2018, we saw more caterpillars and butterflies on our farm than ever," said Frederick, who shares his story at sustainable agriculture meetings across the country. "Pollinator habitat brings us a lot of joy."

Pork and Trees:
Conservation on Iowa's Hog Farms

Conservation can take a variety of forms on Iowa's farms. When Elizabeth Daly of Cedar Rapids heard about a June 2019 field day at a swine farm near Grand Junction, she was willing to drive a few hours to check out how Bruce and Jenny Wessling have incorporated two windbreaks near their finishing barns.

"I'm concerned about environmental degradation and really wanted to see this farm in person," said Daly, a retired Bankers Trust private banking manager who serves as a foundation trustee with Trees Forever, a Marion-based nonprofit organization dedicated to planting trees and encouraging environmental stewardship. "I'm pleased that the Wessling family shows a real concern for the environment."

Trees Forever and the Coalition to Support Iowa's Farmers (CSIF) hosted a field day at the Wesslings' farm in June 2019 to show how livestock producers can utilize trees in windbreaks. Farming in harmony with the environment is important to the Wesslings, who were honored as 2014 Pork Industry Environmental Stewards by the National Pork Board. They've planted hundreds of trees and shrubs, including Norway spruces, cedar trees and austrees (hybrid willows), at their two swine finishing sites since 2009.

"We want to protect water and air quality and live in a healthy environment," said Jenny Wessling, whose family farm provided the first site for the CSIF's Green Farmstead Partner program a decade ago. "Our daughter Jolee and her fiancé, Austin, are planning on staying on the farm, and we want this to continue to be a good place to live."

The Green Farmstead Partner program works with Trees Forever and the Iowa Nursery and Landscape Association to serve livestock farmers

Pork producers Bruce and Jenny Wessling have partnered with Trees Forever and the Coalition to Support Iowa's Farmers to plant hundreds of trees and shrubs on their farm near Grand Junction to protect air and water quality. *Author's collection.*

across Iowa. With the help of twenty-six nursery professionals around the state, this unique initiative provides guidance to farmers who want to plant more trees and shrubs.

Planting trees and shrubs serves as a natural odor filtration system, in addition to beautifying the landscape. Windbreaks have been proven to reduce odor by 10 to 15 percent around livestock barns, according to Iowa State University research. The leaves and needles of the trees capture dust and odor particles, plus trees force air currents upward, causing a tumbling and mixing effect that helps disperse odor.

Iowa producers have planted nearly seventy thousand trees through the Green Farmstead Partner program since it started in 2009. "This is a great example of why a voluntary approach works better than a regulatory approach," said Aaron Putze, senior director of information and education for the Iowa Soybean Association, who spoke at the field day. "Farmers will embrace programs that work and make sense."

Chapter 15

MAKING THE FARM-TO-FORK CONNECTION

G reat food has long been a perk of Iowa farm life. Not only is food one of life's essentials, but it's also a pleasure worth savoring. This was especially true for farm families in years past, when farm life was filled with long days of hard work and few luxuries.

As I sat at his kitchen table a few years ago, visiting about those days gone by, Carroll County farmer Bill Bruggeman recalled how twelve neighborhood families worked together in a threshing ring to harvest oats, a tradition that lasted until the mid-1950s. While Bruggeman's father, Carl, and the other men worked in the field, Bruggeman's mother, Marie, prepared fried chicken, roast beef, mashed potatoes, fruit pies, cream pies and more for dinner to serve the hungry men at noon. "We didn't get electricity on the farm until the 1940s and didn't get running water until the 1950s," added Bruggeman, who noted how hard his mother worked.

The dinner feast was just one meal of the day, however, at threshing time. "Around 5:00 p.m. you'd haul the last load of the day," said Bruggeman, who noted that the farm wives provided the threshing crew with homemade snacks like cookies around 3:00 p.m. "The men were usually served supper, too."

Nobody called these events farm-to-table dinners, as they were just everyday meals. Today, as Iowa has become a much more urbanized society, with nearly two-thirds (64.3 percent) of Iowans in 2016 living in urban areas, according to the Iowa Data Center, farm-to-table dinners have become celebrations of Iowa's food and farming culture.

Threshing and haying time in Iowa meant neighbors worked together (as shown here on the Odland farm in Wright County), and noon meals were homemade feasts of meat, potatoes, pie and more. *Courtesy of Heartland Museum.*

What's old is new again, especially when Leonard and LaVonne Blok hosted a farm-to-table vintage dinner in 2015 to celebrate local foods and heirloom vegetables on their farm near Granville in northwest Iowa. "Be prepared for the wow factor," said Leonard Blok, as he described the flavors of his favorite heirloom tomatoes and heirloom vegetables. "This is why grandma's cooking tasted so good."

The Bloks are keeping these traditions alive at Heirloom Acres south of Granville, where they welcomed more than forty guests on September 17, 2015, to their farm-to-table vintage dinner. Before dinner, guests were encouraged to tour the gardens filled with heirloom vegetables of all types. They could also pick apples from the orchard on the farm.

The Bloks' sense of humor and love of gardening inspire their passion to grow fresh food on their acreage. They've planted nearly ninety heirloom tomato plants (totaling thirty-one different varieties) in recent years in their spacious "Garden of Eatin."

The Bloks partnered with local friends, neighbors and Iowa State University Extension to offer a taste of northwest Iowa during their farm-to-table dinner, which included wine tasting and live music at Heirloom Acres. The menu featured Roasted Garlic Alfredo Vegetable Lasagna, Kale and Beet Salad, Cabbage Salad and more. "The Bloks did a great

Leonard and LaVonne Blok hosted a farm-to-table vintage dinner in 2015 on their farm near Granville to celebrate local foods and heirloom vegetables. *Author's collection.*

job of entertaining and offering unique, fresh flavors," said Fran Peelen, whose family farms in the Sanborn area. "This farm-to-fork experience was wonderful."

KALE AND BEET SALAD

This salad was served at the Granville farm-to-table dinner. It can be made with heirloom "Vates Dwarf Blue" or "Redbor" kale and heirloom "Cylindra" beets. The beets can be prepped several days in advance. This salad holds up well ahead of serving.

4 beets, approximately 2.5 inches in size
1 bunch curly type kale
¼ medium red onion, sliced thin

Dressing:
2 tablespoons olive oil
4 tablespoons balsamic vinegar

1 teaspoon brown mustard
2 tablespoons honey
3 tablespoons orange juice

Topping:
¼ cup cashews
feta cheese crumbles

Place washed beets in a 3-quart sauce pot. Leave root tip and 3 inches of stem on beets to prevent bleeding. Cover with water. Bring to a full boil. Cover pot with lid. Turn off heat. Go to bed. In the morning, drain off water, slip skins and shred or slice the beets.

Wash kale. Cover with boiling water for 30 seconds. Drain. Rinse in cold water; drain again. Tear into bite-sized pieces.

Whisk olive oil, balsamic vinegar, brown mustard, honey and orange juice together. Toss dressing with kale, beets and onion. Sprinkle salad with cashews and feta cheese.

Burger Bragging Rights

Another fun celebration of the farm-to-fork connection is the Best Burger in Iowa contest. Each year since 2010, Iowa's cattle producers have asked their fellow Iowans to help find Iowa's Best Burger, whether it's gourmet or down-home.

The popular contest, which is sponsored by the Iowa Beef Industry Council (IBIC) and Iowa Cattlemen's Association (ICA), attracts thousands of nominations each year. The first phase is all based on votes from the public. For a month, burger lovers go online and vote for their favorite Iowa burger. Burger fans submitted nearly ten thousand votes in 2018, representing about seven hundred restaurants.

The ten restaurants with the most votes are eligible for the title of Iowa's Best Burger. To qualify to be named Iowa's Best Burger, the burger must be a 100 percent beef burger and served on a bun or bread product. An anonymous panel of judges will visit each of the ten restaurants to judge the burgers on appearance, taste and proper cooking temperature (160 degrees Fahrenheit) to determine the winner, which is showcased during May Beef Month.

If you win the Best Burger in Iowa award, be prepared for an onslaught of new business, and hope that your loyal customers remain patient. Just ask Claudio Gianello, who saw how guests flocked from all across Iowa and beyond and filled every table in Café Beaudelaire in Ames after the café won the 2018 Best Burger in Iowa contest. "We were excited to kick off May Beef Month by awarding Café Beaudelaire with the title of the Best Burger in Iowa," said Brooke German, director of marketing for IBIC. "The Brazilian-inspired restaurant serves a hand-pattied burger, and the judges noted that the taste and quality of the burger is outstanding and worth a drive to have it again."

HOG HEAVEN: IOWA KNOWS ALL THINGS PORK

Just as Iowans love a great beef burger, it's hard to think of Iowa without thinking of pork. After all, Iowa has long been the nation's top pork-producing state.

Thousands of people visit the famous Pork Tent at the Iowa State Fair each year to enjoy pork chops on a stick and more. The Pork Tent, where pork producers from across Iowa volunteer to grill the meat, has also become a premier photo opportunity for politicians of all types, including presidential hopefuls.

Don't forget Iowa's famous breaded tenderloins. Since 2003, the Iowa Pork Producers Association (IPPA) has sponsored the Iowa's Best Tenderloin contest. While most of the winners have been breaded tenderloins, at least one winner was a grilled tenderloin. Interest in the contest continues to grow. In 2019, IPPA received 5,390 nominations for 470 different establishments during the nomination period.

Iowa's Best Tenderloin judges evaluate tenderloins on the quality of the pork, taste, physical characteristics and eating experience. "Ultimately, we're looking for a sandwich that showcases pork first and is complemented with a flavorful breading," said Chef Phil Carey, who has helped judge the contest.

Want to create your own version of a classic Iowa pork tenderloin? Try this one from my friend Jenny Unternahrer from southeast Iowa, who writes the blog *In the Kitchen with Jenny*:

Breaded Pork Tenderloins

1 cup flour (divided)
1 egg
½ cup milk
approximately ½ sleeve saltine crackers (crushed)
3–4 boneless pork loin chops, tenderized
lard (or canola oil), enough for about ½ to ¾ of an inch in bottom of pan

Set up your breading stations. One with ½ cup flour, one with the egg and milk mixed and the other with the crackers and other ½ cup of flour mixed. (You can season your breading if you like with salt or seasoning salt.)

Dip your tenderloin in the flour. Coat on both sides. Dip in egg/milk mixture. Coat with cracker/flour mixture, gently pressing into the tenderloin so it sticks. Fry in hot oil/lard approximately 3–4 minutes on each side until cooked through.

Drain on paper towels. Serve on buns with desired condiments, including mustard, mayonnaise, dill pickle chips, ketchup, sliced onion, lettuce and tomato. Tenderloins can also be cut into strips and dipped in ketchup.

Fresh Produce Abounds in Iowa

Iowa's farm-to-fork connection includes much more than meat-and-potatoes meals. There are some foods so Iowan that they hardly need explanation, like fresh Iowa sweet corn.

Various towns across the state host sweet corn celebrations each summer, including the Adel Sweet Corn Festival, which celebrated its fortieth anniversary in 2019. More than seven tons of locally grown sweet corn were husked, cooked and given away for free to the hundreds of people who attend the annual event in Adel, the Dallas County seat in central Iowa.

Delicacies like ears of sweet corn wrapped in bacon also offer a distinctive taste of Iowa each summer at various food vendor stands in small towns along the Register's Annual Great Bicycle Ride Across Iowa (RAGBRAI), which has been showcasing rural Iowa to people nationwide since 1973. It's truly a moveable feast for the more than ten thousand bicycle riders who work up quite an appetite as they pedal nearly five hundred miles across rural Iowa for a week in late July.

There are some foods so Iowan that they hardly need explanation, like fresh Iowa sweet corn. Various towns across the state host sweet corn celebrations each summer, including Adel. *Author's collection.*

JOLLY TIME INFLUENCES "POP" CULTURE

Much like RAGBRAI, food, family and fun have also created a trifecta of success for Sioux City's JOLLY TIME Pop Corn, which celebrated its 100th anniversary in 2014. "Our greatest joy and constant motivation is bringing families and friends together," said Garry Smith, company president and fourth generation of the Smith family to lead JOLLY TIME Pop Corn.

JOLLY TIME was founded in 1914 in Sioux City, where Cloid Smith and his son, Howard, hand-shelled popcorn in the basement of their home. An entrepreneur at heart, Cloid Smith pioneered the U.S. popcorn industry, starting with sales to small grocers and street-cart popcorn vendors.

Through the years, JOLLY TIME's product lines have evolved in the ever-changing snack food market. The 1980s, for example, brought the advent of microwave popcorn. The early 2000s led to the creation of new popcorn varieties for more health-conscious snacking.

Today, JOLLY TIME offers its American-grown products in grocery stores nationwide and in nearly forty countries. It's still based at its "One Fun

Place" street address in Sioux City and remains a family-owned business. "We have a good time reaching our goal of capturing a bigger piece of the market in many different places," Smith said.

DOWNTOWN FARMERS' MARKET GAINS NATIONAL ACCLAIM

Businesses is also popping at farmers' markets across Iowa, including the nationally renowned Downtown Farmers' Market in downtown Des Moines. Since it was established in 1976, the Downtown Farmers' Market has become the oldest, continuously operating farmers' market in America.

In 2013 and 2014, the Downtown Farmers' Market ranked near the top of the best 101 farmers' markets in America by the *Daily Meal*. Covering thirteen city blocks, the market attracts twenty thousand people each Saturday morning, on average, from May through October. The market has become a premier shopping destination for fresh food and unique items. In 2016, more than three hundred local entrepreneurs including farmers, producers, bakers, artists and more representing fifty-eight counties across Iowa were selling at the market.

No two markets are ever alike, said Kelly Foss, market director. "That's the charm of the farmers' market. There are always new flavors as the seasons change, and there's something for everybody."

DELICIOUS APPLES, A MADISON COUNTY ORIGINAL

Home-grown Iowa apples are always a favorite each fall, from farmers' markets to apple orchards across the state. Over the years, Iowa horticulturists have developed new types of apples that have appealed to a wide range of tastes.

Among these horticulturists were Jesse and Rebecca Hiatt, who arrived in Madison County about 150 years ago with a wagon full of fruit trees. They moved into a small log cabin on a hill north of the tiny town of Peru and planted an orchard. Around 1872, Jesse Hiatt (1826–1898) noticed a little sprout growing up between his straight rows of apple trees. He decided it didn't belong there, so he cut down the sprout. The unusual little seedling kept coming back, however, even after Hiatt cut it down several times. He decided to nurture the determined little tree and found that its first fruit had not only a crispy, juicy texture but also a remarkable flavor.

Hiatt named it "Hawkeye," after his adopted state where the new apple was born. For years, he promoted his new fruit to area residents. He also took his Hawkeye apples to county fairs to be judged. Other apples earned blue ribbons, but not Hiatt's Hawkeye, according to "The Best Apple in the World," which appeared in the May 1, 2019, issue of the *Winterset Madisonian*.

Undeterred, Hiatt took a crate of his Hawkeye apples to the local train station and shipped his new fruit to Missouri in 1893 to the International New Fruit Fair hosted by Stark Bros. Nursery in Louisiana, Missouri. Upon biting into the apple, one judge proclaimed it "delicious," and that name stuck. Stark Bros. Nursery later asked for permission to purchase the rights to propagate the Hawkeye apples. Hiatt agreed. The Delicious apple would become world famous and change the apple industry forever.

A descendant of the original Delicious apple tree still stands just north of Peru in Madison County, according to the Madison County Chamber of Commerce.

LIVING HISTORY FARMS AND THE MACHINE SHED

Apples form the basis of some of the most popular desserts and sweetbreads at the Machine Shed Restaurant, which has two Iowa locations, including Davenport and Urbandale.

Throughout the year, the Machine Shed restaurant offers an authentic taste of Iowa farm cooking. In 1978, the first Machine Shed Restaurant opened on the outskirts of Davenport. As the business has expanded and evolved, all Machine Shed restaurants remain dedicated to the American farmer. That's why Machine Shed restaurants proudly proclaim the message "Farming Is Everyone's Bread and Butter."

It's a perfect fit for the Machine Shed in Urbandale, which is located right next to Living History Farms (LHF). For more than forty years, Living History Farms has told the amazing story of how Iowans transformed the fertile midwestern prairies into the most productive farmland in the world. LHF includes an Ioway village, an 1850 pioneer farm, an 1875 town of Walnut Hill and a 1900 farm. Living History Farms also hosts historic

In 1978, the first Machine Shed Restaurant opened on the outskirts of Davenport. As the business has expanded to Urbandale and other communities, all Machine Shed restaurants remain dedicated to the American farmer. *Courtesy of the Iowa Machine Shed.*

dinners during the winter, where guests can sample traditional Iowa fare at the 1900 farm or the 1875 Tangen House.

As heritage tourism grows in popularity nationwide, LHF is spurring economic development in Urbandale. In 2018, the museum welcomed eighty-three thousand visitors from all fifty states and seventeen countries. Guests who work up an appetite can stop by the Machine Shed for a hearty helping of farm-inspired, midwestern comfort food daily. Here's a recipe for a Machine Shed classic:

Applesauce Sweet Bread

3 cups all-purpose flour
1½ teaspoons baking soda
1 teaspoon salt
1 cup butter, softened
1½ cups sugar
3 eggs
¼ cup evaporated milk or milk

1 teaspoon vanilla
1 ½ cups applesauce
2 tablespoons cinnamon-sugar

Grease the bottom and ½ an inch up the sides of two 8x4x2-inch loaf pans; set aside. In a medium bowl combine flour, soda and salt. Set aside.

In a large mixing bowl, beat butter with an electric mixer on medium to high speed for 30 seconds. Add sugar; beat until well combined. Beat in eggs, milk and vanilla. Beat in applesauce. Beat in flour mix until combined.

Divide mixture between prepared pans. Sprinkle tops of each with cinnamon-sugar. Bake at 325 degrees for 60 minutes, or until a toothpick inserted near the centers comes out clean. Cool in pans on a wire rack for 10 minutes. Remove from pans. Cool completely.

SEED SAVERS, ONEOTA COMMUNITY FOOD CO-OP THRIVE IN DECORAH

Preserving a taste of Iowa's rural heritage also guides Seed Savers Exchange, which has provided a unique resource for food lovers and gardeners for decades. Located on 890 scenic acres in Winneshiek County near Decorah, Seed Savers Exchange has protected the biodiversity of our food system—and our planet—for nearly fifty years by preserving rare, heirloom and open-pollinated varieties of seeds and encouraging gardeners and farmers worldwide to grow, harvest and share heirloom seeds, as well as recount the inspirational stories behind them.

It was her own children's future that inspired Diane Ott Whealy to cofound Seed Savers Exchange with Kent Whealy. Diane's grandfather had entrusted to the pair with the seeds of two garden plants, including the "German Pink" tomato and "Grandpa Ott's morning glory." These seeds, brought by Grandpa Ott's parents from Bavaria to Iowa in the 1870s, became the first two varieties in the collection. Diane and Kent Whaley went on to form a network of gardeners interested in preserving heirloom varieties and sharing seeds.

"We built a movement, not a seed company," notes the Seed Savers website. "Since 1975, we have been working hard to keep heirloom varieties where they belong—in our gardens, on our tables and in our hearts."

Since 1975, Seed Savers Exchange near Decorah has protected the biodiversity of the food system by preserving rare, heirloom and open-pollinated varieties of seeds. *Author's collection.*

Decorah is also home to the Oneota Community Food Co-op, where they say that "local and organic aren't just a corner of our store—they are the cornerstone of our cooperative business." The Oneota Community Food Co-op is a cooperatively owned grocery store specializing in organic, local and sustainably produced products since 1974. With more than five thousand member-owners, the co-op has become a hub of activity in the community.

The Oneota Community Food Co-op's mission? Build vibrant communities and ecosystems by providing organic, locally produced and bulk foods, as well as other products and services that are sustainable for those who consume and produce them.

In its 2017 annual report, the Oneota Community Food Co-op reported annual sales of more than $5.1 million, fifty-seven employees and more than $7,500 in total donations contributed to the community. "It is no secret to those who love our co-op that we have created something more than a grocery store," noted Brita Nelson, board president.

Ultra-Local Eating through Community-Supported Agriculture

Jennifer Miller, who farms in the Waukee area, is also passionate about local food and creating a sense of community. Still, she could hardly believe the question she was asked. "When will your bananas be ready?" inquired a central Iowa woman who was buying fresh produce through Miller's Clarion Sage market garden and community-supported agriculture (CSA) business.

"People are disconnected from where their food comes from," said Miller, who noted the woman seeking locally grown bananas was a well-educated business professional. "I've even had people look at our heirloom tomatoes and say, 'I don't want those,' because they think they are GMOs [genetically modified organisms]."

This disconnect isn't all that foreign to Miller, who grew up in Highland Park, Illinois, a northern suburb of Chicago. "I had no contact with agriculture in Highland Park," said Miller, who has served as the Iowa Food Cooperative's member services coordinator.

After moving to Iowa, Miller got involved with community gardens in the Des Moines area and became a marketing/communications specialist for Iowa Food Cooperative, which operates like an online farmers' market. In 2013, Miller and her partner, Cody Kilgore, moved to an acreage on the southwest edge of Waukee's city limits in Van Meter Township so they could operate their own farm.

The couple planted garlic in the fall of 2013 to start their Clarion Sage market garden. They raise a wide array of vegetables and herbs, including lettuce, squash, cabbage, carrots, garlic, tomatoes, cucumbers, peppers, potatoes and more, including heirloom varieties that can't be found in most stores. "Food can be so much more interesting," Miller said. "Whether you're sharing a family meal, providing snacks for your kids or making a favorite recipe, one thing's for sure: the starting point for all these is good food."

Iowa Uncorked: Grape, Wine Industries Mature in Iowa

Good wine enhances good food. Grape-growing is nothing new in Iowa's ag history. Iowa ranked eleventh in grape production in the United States in 1899, according to the Iowa Wine Growers Association. By 1919, Iowa was the sixth-largest wine producer in the nation.

Nearly one hundred licensed wineries operate in Iowa, including Rustic River Winery north of Lake View. Eight official wine trails crisscross the state, spurring tourism and economic development. *Author's collection.*

Prohibition, more row-crop production, a severe blizzard in 1940 and other factors diminished the number of grapes grown in Iowa. Iowa's wine and grape industry has rebounded in recent years, with the full economic impact of Iowa wine and wine grapes totaling $420 million in 2012, according to Iowa State University.

Between 1990 and 2000, Iowa only had approximately 30 acres of grapes in production and thirteen wineries. Fast-forward to today, where nearly one hundred licensed wineries are operating in Iowa and nearly three hundred commercial vineyards cover more than 1,300 acres across the state, according to the Iowa Wine Growers Association.

Eight official wine trails crisscross the state. Wine-related tourism expenditures jumped more than 51 percent from 2008 to 2012, rising from $27 million to $41 million, according to Iowa State University. "Wineries continue to spread their footprint as they expand into event centers, bed-and-breakfasts, restaurants, wedding venues and more," said Michael White, Iowa State University's viticulture specialist.

Norm and Marsha Phillips, who farm north of Lake View in west-central Iowa, remodeled their old barn to become the hub of their Rustic

River Winery. Perched on a gently rolling hill, the iconic barn overlooks the family's vineyard and has created a new destination for locals and visitors in Sac County. "Our niche is that we're a small, family-owned winery doing things the old-fashioned way," said Marsha Phillips, whose family planted their first grapevines in 2009. "The most fun part is meeting people, including other winemakers."

Chapter 16

THE FUTURE OF IOWA AGRICULTURE

If you eat, you have a connection to farming every day. While decades of Iowa agriculture have shaped modern farming, the story is far from over. This dynamic industry continues to evolve, especially as Iowa farmers grow in new directions while staying focused on continuous improvement.

"Iowa's ag history isn't just something that happened long ago and far away," said Julie Kenney, who grew up on a farm near Lohrville in west-central Iowa and serves as Iowa's deputy secretary of agriculture. "It touches our lives every day, from the food we eat to the biofuels that power our vehicles. It's valuable to rediscover what shaped modern Iowa and how agriculture is intertwined not only with our past, but our future."

Strong ag leaders from Iowa have helped chart this course for generations. "Tama Jim" James Wilson (1835–1920), a farmer from Tama County, served as a state lawmaker, U.S. representative for three terms and head of Iowa State College's Agricultural Experiment Station and Professor of Agriculture (the title that was used before the title "Dean of Agriculture" came into existence) before serving as the U.S. secretary of agriculture from 1897 to 1913. He served during the presidential administrations of William McKinley, Theodore Roosevelt and William Howard Taft.

"Some historians consider Wilson the greatest of all U.S. secretaries of agriculture," noted the Biographical Dictionary of Iowa. "During his tenure…the agricultural balance of trade increased from $23 million to almost $425 million; the value of farm products expanded more than 200 percent; and the number of farms [nationwide] grew from 4.6 million to 6.1 million."

Four other Iowans would serve as U.S. Department of Agriculture secretary, including Edwin Meredith, who founded *Successful Farming* magazine and served as ag secretary from 1920 to 1921; Henry Cantwell Wallace, editor of *Wallaces' Farmer*, who served from 1921 to 1924; Wallace's son, Henry A. Wallace, who served from 1933 to 1940; and Tom Vilsack, who served from 2009 to 2017.

Three of these men were among the longest-serving U.S. ag secretaries in history, including Wilson (sixteen years of service), Henry A. Wallace (more than seven years) and Vilsack (more than seven years).

ETHANOL POWERS NEW OPPORTUNITIES

Before he was named U.S. secretary of agriculture, Vilsack served as the fortieth governor of Iowa from 1999 to 2007, a time when the biofuels industry accelerated tremendously in Iowa. One of the most visible examples of the renewable fuels industry in Iowa is corn-based ethanol, whose roots go back to the 1970s.

"The ethanol industry got started by visionaries who were tired of being held captive to low corn prices and wanted to find a way to write their own ticket," said Mark Heckman, a farmer from West Liberty and former chairman of the Iowa Corn Promotion Board (ICPB). He helped promote ethanol during the Iowa Corn 300 race at the Iowa Speedway in Newton on July 9, 2017—the year the Iowa Corn Growers Association (ICGA) celebrated the group's fiftieth anniversary.

Those visionary farmers who supported ethanol early on included Thurman Gaskill, a Corwith farmer who served as ICPB's first president in 1978. When this future ICGA president and state senator pumped Iowa's first tank of corn-based ethanol (called gasohol back then) in the eastern Iowa town of Clarence, many people viewed this new fuel as just a corn-fed gimmick.

Iowa corn growers like Gaskill were undeterred in their quest to provide a solution to the 1970s energy crisis and low corn prices. Iowa Corn leaders found five filling stations willing to sell gasoline mixed with 10 percent ethanol in Clarence, Cumberland, Osage, Peterson and Fort Dodge.

Today, Iowa has forty-three ethanol refineries with 4.5 billion gallons of annual production capacity, according to the Iowa Renewable Fuels

Association. That equates to more than 1 billion bushels of corn demand. In fact, 39 percent of Iowa's corn crop is used for ethanol fuel, according to Iowa Corn. A portion of the corn used for ethanol is also turned into a co-product called distillers dried grains (DDGs), a high protein, valuable livestock feed. "The 15.3 billion gallons of ethanol used in 2016 reduced greenhouse gas emissions by a whopping 43.5 million metric tons," Iowa Corn added. "That's like removing 9.3 million cars from the road."

Biodiesel Benefits the Economy and Environment

Corn-based ethanol isn't the only ag biofuel that helps power Iowa's rural economy today. Biodisel, which can be made from soybeans, is also important. There are eleven biodiesel plants throughout Iowa, according to the Iowa Biodiesel Board (IBB).

Iowa biodiesel producers made about 365 million gallons of biodiesel in 2018, according to the National Biodiesel Board. This makes Iowa the leading biodiesel-producing state.

For Des Moines–based Ruan Transportation, the decision to use biodiesel from the Renewable Energy Group (REG), LLC, which has a location in Ames, was simple. "It's well known that transportation is one of the largest contributors to emissions in the country," said Steve Larsen, director of procurement and fuel for Ruan Transportation, which has nearly 4,000 semi-tractors and 9,500 trailers that travel roughly 350 million miles in forty-eight states per year. "If we can improve our performance in a manner that can help that problem, we're glad to do so."

Biodiesel plants across Iowa are also finding new ways to protect the environment. In 2019, the Western Iowa Energy biodiesel plant near Wall Lake joined the Monarch Fueling Station Project. The Monarch Fueling Station Project, which the Iowa Renewable Fuels Association launched in December 2017 in partnership with the Iowa Monarch Conservation Consortium, is helping restore monarch habitat across rural Iowa in the heart of the monarch butterfly migration path.

"We transform agriculture coproducts into green fuel," said Kevin Bieret, operations manager for Western Iowa Energy. "We see this Monarch Fueling Project as a new way to do that again, by turning something we have to mow into habitat to help fuel monarch butterflies."

HARNESSING WIND AND SOLAR POWER

Rural Iowa is also leading the way in other renewable energy options. In 2017, Iowa ranked first in the nation in terms of wind power generation relative to total in-state electricity production, according to the Iowa Farm Bureau Federation.

By 2019, there were 4,145 wind turbines across the state, according to the Iowa Wind Energy Association. Iowa generated 20.82 million megawatt-hours from wind power in 2017 and contributed 37 percent of the state's electricity supply.

Rural areas in Iowa are also harnessing the power of the sun to generate electricity. In the summer of 2017, the Calhoun County REC installed a new seventy-six-kilowatt demonstration and education project solar array east of its office in Rockwell City. Solar arrays are also being installed on Iowa farms.

Dwight Dial—a corn, soybean, hog and sheep producer from Lake City—assessed his electrical usage data from the past three years so a solar company could determine how many kilowatts would be required to power Dial's home and farm. "It was a great day when we flipped the switch to solar," said Dial, who has received the Iowa Department of Agriculture and Land Stewardship's (IDALS) Environmental Leader Award.

CELEBRATING IOWA'S GOOD FARM NEIGHBORS

Honoring farmers who do the right things to protect the environment is reflected in programs like the Wergin Good Farm Neighbor Award, which recognizes Iowa livestock farmers who take pride in doing things right and go above and beyond as environmental stewards and animal caretakers.

The award, presented by the Iowa Department of Agriculture and Land Stewardship and Iowa Ag Radio Network, is made possible through the financial support of the Coalition to Support Iowa's Farmers. It's named in memory of Gary Wergin (1955–2004), a longtime WHO Radio farm broadcaster.

"Animal agriculture is so important to our state and adds so much to rural communities," said Mike Naig, Iowa secretary of agriculture. "It's an honor to help recognize our farm families who do such a great job caring for their animals and protecting the environment while also being active leaders in the community and helping feed the world."

The Wergin Good Farm Neighbor Award recognizes Iowa livestock farmers who go above and beyond as environmental stewards and animal caretakers. The Folsom family, who raise hogs, corn and soybeans near Rockwell City, won this award in 2018. *Author's collection.*

Do You Know the Farmer Wave?

Perhaps nowhere is this spirit of "Iowa nice" from a good neighbor more obvious than the now-famous "farmer wave." "If Iowa had its own 10 commandments of rural driving, one of the holy laws handed down from brittle scrolls excavated out of an ancient barn would read: 'Thou shalt raise a finger or two off thy pickup steering wheel as a friendly greeting to fellow farmers,'" wrote Kyle Munson in the November 11, 2014 *Des Moines Register* article "'Farmer Wave Week' Celebrates Rural Ritual of the Finger Salute."

Yes, there is a rural ritual known as the "farmer wave." But Todd Collins had no idea the cultural tsunami he was about to unleash when on a whim he launched his grass-roots campaign to establish "Farmer Wave Week" in Iowa, Munson wrote. In 2014, that idea became official when then governor Terry Branstad signed a proclamation to recognize the first Farmer Wave Week.

Farmer Wave Week "encourages all Iowans to display their Midwestern hospitality and extend this simple, friendly gesture to all that they might meet." The cultural message of the farmer wave, Collins explained, is almost like saying, "I trust you, you're a good person."

Collins, who grew up on a farm near Carroll, Iowa, said the farmer wave was an everyday occurrence. It wasn't until he moved to Wisconsin, however, that Collins noticed that only in Iowa did he see the farmer wave on a regular basis. "You would be amazed at what a simple farmer wave can do to make someone's day," said Collins in an interview with the Iowa Farm Bureau Federation.

Collins contacted the staff of then Iowa agriculture secretary Bill Northey with his idea. They suggested he submit a request for an official state proclamation declaring "Farmer Wave Week." Less than twenty-four hours later, Collins found out that Branstad had approved his request. The governor proclaimed November 9–15, 2014, as Farmer Wave Week in Iowa. This proud tradition continues today.

Cultivating Community: Dogpatch Urban Gardens Thrive in Des Moines

While you may not see the farmer wave in Iowa's urban areas, that doesn't mean agriculture isn't alive and well in the heart of the city. Consider Dogpatch Urban Gardens in Des Moines. While cars zip by on a busy thoroughfare, an oasis filled with row after row of vegetables flourishes on the small farm. "I've always had my own garden," noted farm owner Jenny Quiner, who began operating her urban farm with her husband, Eric, in 2015. "Now we have an acre here in the city."

Quiner and her family have transformed a once-vacant space at the corner of Meredith Drive and Northwest Fifty-First Street into a destination filled with gardens covering a quarter of an acre, a high-tunnel greenhouse that was added in 2017, open space for events and a farm stand where customers can buy fresh garden produce and other locally produced items from May to November.

Quiner, who grew up in Urbandale, describes Dogpatch Urban Gardens as a family-run farm focused on health, community, education and the environment. She cultivates fresh, nutritious, flavorful produce in the northern Beaverdale area of Des Moines using organic, biointensive farming methods to produce high yields on a minimal amount of land while maintaining the integrity of the environment. "Do I think my style of urban farming can feed the world? No. But do I think this type of farming can enhance a community, spark conversations about use of our natural resources, enhance soil health and inspire others? Yes."

OLD SCHOOL TO BOLD SCHOOL:
GILMORE CITY-BRADGATE EMBRACES
SEED-TO-TABLE LEARNING

Step into the elementary school lunchroom in Gilmore City around noon and be prepared for a steady patter of tennis shoes, the low roar of children's voices echoing from the doorway to the stage and enthusiastic comments like, "Yeah, carrots!" when the students see the salad bar.

"We teach our students to be the best they can be, and a big part of that is being healthy and eating right," said Kelsey Wigans, a registered dietitian who has served as the first seed-to-table garden manager at the Gilmore City–Bradgate Elementary School since 2016.

To the best of her knowledge, Wigans is the only seed-to-table garden manager working full-time in a public school in Iowa. This unique role allows her to serve the 135 children at the Gilmore City school, including students from preschool through sixth grade. Various learning opportunities abound on about an acre and a half of land, from the greenhouse near the bus barn to container gardens and an orchard just north of the school.

"When we started this a few years ago, only about 10 percent of students ate vegetables from the salad bar," said Wigans, who adds a drizzle of ranch dressing to each child's lunch tray if he or she wants a little extra flavor on their vegetables. "Now nearly half of the kids eat the veggies."

All these opportunities boost students' ag literacy—a critical component for a well-rounded education, emphasize school leaders. "Even though Iowa has some of the most fertile farm ground in the world, so many people are disconnected from agriculture and food production," said Wigans, who grew up on a corn, soybean and cattle farm in central Iowa. "I love helping people connect the dots between farming, food and nutrition."

It All Starts with the Seed

Adults can immerse themselves in modern farming and food production at the Huxley Learning Center, which opened in 2014.

Tours start in the Seed Science hallway, where visitors learn about the basics of plant genetics. "The future of farming has arrived," said Charles Boateng, PhD, a Huxley Learning Center agronomist. "We want to help give people a whole new appreciation for modern agriculture."

Consider Bt corn, a genetically modified organism (GMO) that includes genes from a naturally occurring soil bacterium, *Bacillus thuringiensis* (Bt), that produces proteins with insecticidal properties. Some Bt corn hybrids help protect plants against European corn borers, while some protect against corn rootworms.

"When I hold up stalks and roots from corn with Bt and without Bt, people who don't know a lot about farming are shocked when they compare the healthy root system to the one that has been destroyed by insects," said Boateng, who explains how a strong root system is vital for the uptake of nutrients and water that keep plants healthy. "This is a big ah-ha moment."

Traits like Bt have helped reduce pesticide use in agricultural production by 1 billion pounds since 1996, when the first biotech traits came on the market, Boateng added. "In terms of the environmental impact, that's like taking 11.8 million cars off the road for a year."

The Huxley Learning Center also explains the role of management zones and digital ag solutions that provide data to help farmers make better decisions throughout the growing season. Part of precision ag today includes grid soil sampling, where soil samples are collected throughout the field to test nutrient levels. The results can be used to write prescriptions for variable-rate fertilizer applications. Instead of blanketing a field with the same amount of fertilizer everywhere, variable-rate application means more nutrients are placed where soil fertility levels are low, while fewer or no nutrients are applied where fertility levels are higher. All this helps protect water quality.

Real-time connectivity in the tractor or combine cab, combined with cloud-to-cloud data transfers, have also ushered in a new era of farming. By analyzing data gathered from sensors to satellites, farmers are using tablet computers, smartphone apps and more to select the right seed genetics, plan fertilizer use, track crop health and measure yields to improve the efficiency of their businesses like never before.

"Digital agriculture is the next wave of innovation that's transforming agriculture," Boateng said.

IOWA FOOD & FAMILY PROJECT CONNECTS RURAL, URBAN

Iowa agriculture offers something for everyone, especially when it comes to exploring and enjoying the bounty of Iowa. The Ankeny-based Iowa Food & Family Project invites people to discover how food is grown around the state and meet the farmers who make it happen—24/7, 365 days a year.

"At the Iowa Food & Family Project we're all about celebrating farm families, uniting rural and urban communities and providing the information and experiences you need to make informed food choices," said Kelly Visser, consumer engagement manager.

The Iowa Food & Family Project is a presenting sponsor of Live Healthy Iowa, a program of the Iowa Sports Foundation that encourages team-based challenges to promote positive lifestyle changes. The Iowa Food & Family Project includes a network of nearly thirty-five food, farming and healthy living organizations that are proud of Iowa's homegrown foods and hometown values. The Iowa Food & Family Project hosts a number of activities throughout the year that connect farmers and nonfarmers,

The Iowa Food and Family Project hosts Expedition Farm Country to connect people who don't live on farms with Iowa farmers. During this annual two-day event, forty to fifty participants tour farms (such as the Dougherty Century Farm near Yetter, shown here in 2015) and have honest conversations about modern agriculture. *Author's collection.*

including educational events at the Iowa State Fair and Food for Thought dialogues involving farmers, members of the public and noted food writers.

Each summer, the Iowa Food & Family Project hosts Expedition Farm Country, which attracts participants from across Iowa and beyond. "During the two-day adventure, you'll have the opportunity to meet farm families and learn firsthand how food is grown and raised," notes the Iowa Food & Family Project. "Enjoy local eateries, historic sites and the best of farm life along the way."

IOWA CELEBRATES CENTURY FARMS, HERITAGE FARMS

Expedition Farm Country tours often include visits to some of Iowa's Century Farms and Heritage Farms. The Century Farms Program, which is coordinated by the Iowa Department of Agriculture and Land Stewardship (IDALS), honors people who have owned the same piece of farmland for one hundred years or more.

The program began in 1976 as part of America's bicentennial celebration, when more than five thousand Century Farm certificates signs were distributed across Iowa. Since then, more than fifteen thousand families have been recognized during a special ceremony that's held each year at the Iowa State Fair. In recent years, IDALS and the Iowa Farm Bureau Federation established the Heritage Farm Program for farm families who have owned at least forty acres for 150 years or more.

"When you consider all the challenges that previous generations went through, you have an even greater appreciation for a Century Farm," said Dave Klocke, a Templeton-area farmer whose family received a Century Farm award in 2017. "The potential to make the farm even more productive keeps me motivated."

JUST PRESS PLAY: AMES COMPANY UNVEILS DRIVERLESS TRACTOR TECHNOLOGY

While the Century Farm and Heritage Farm awards honor the past, the Farm Progress Show is focused on the future. As the nation's largest outdoor farm event, the show annually hosts more than six hundred exhibitors and attracts hundreds of thousands of visitors from across the United States and around the globe.

The show, which dates back to the early 1950s, has been held at various locations across Iowa. Now it rotates between its two permanent sites: Decatur, Illinois, and Boone, Iowa.

In 2018, an Iowa tech company made Farm Progress Show history with its autonomous tractor demonstration, an event that attracted national media attention and offered a glimpse into the future of agriculture. "When you see this, you feel there's something really big going on," said Mark Barglof, chief technical officer for Ames-based Smart Ag, which showcased an aftermarket kit for driverless tractors during field demonstrations at the 2018 Farm Progress Show near Boone.

Smart Ag debuted AutoCart®, a software application that fully automates a grain cart tractor and can provide farmers with much-needed labor assistance during harvest. The result of two and a half years of development, AutoCart and the tractor aftermarket kit offer a simple plug-and-play system.

The technology allows farmers to automate their existing equipment and maximize their capacity and efficiency. As the first cloud-based platform for driverless tractors, this system can help address the issues of labor and productivity for today's farmers, said Colin Hurd, Smart Ag's founder and CEO, who earned his degree in agriculture and business from Iowa State University in 2013. "If there's one thing the Farm Progress Show has taught us over its sixty-five-year history, it's that agriculture is at its best when farmers have choices."

Hollywood Shines the Spotlight on Rural Iowa

Agriculture doesn't capture the spotlight only during the Farm Progress Show. Iowa agriculture has also starred in a variety of blockbuster Hollywood movies in the past thirty years, from *The Bridges of Madison County* to *Field of Dreams*.

In June 2019, the *Field of Dreams* movie site celebrated the thirtieth anniversary of one of the most beloved baseball films of all time. To understand the significance of this event, it's important to roll back the clock to the late 1980s. The farm crisis was just starting to loosen its chokehold on rural Iowa. One cold day in eastern Iowa in late December 1987, a volunteer named Sue Riedel with the Dubuque Chamber of Commerce (working in conjunction with the Iowa Film Board) knocked on the door of a farmhouse near Dyersville.

Don Lansing answered. "We're thinking of making a movie in the area on a farm," Riedel told Lansing, the third generation of his family to live on the farm. "It possibly could be your farm. Would you allow us to take a video?"

A chain of events in the next few months would culminate in Lansing signing a contract for the use of his farm for the filming of *Shoeless Joe*. It took about nineteen weeks to film the movie, whose title was later changed to *Field of Dreams*. Since then, the movie has gained accolades worldwide and has made Dyersville a popular tourist destination for young and old alike. (Dyersville is also home to the National Farm Toy Museum.)

The film connects with anyone longing to be a part of something greater than themselves. "This movie is about redemption, second chances, pursuing your dreams and giving back," said Roman Weinberg, operations manager for Go the Distance Baseball, LLC, which operates the *Field of Dreams* movie site.

People continue to be drawn to the site. In the past decade, eighty-five to ninety thousand people visit the site each year. "This movie transcends culture and language barriers," said Weinberg, who noted that guests hail from Japan, Australia, England and beyond.

It's a wonderful thing for Iowa, added Weinberg, who grew up in Dubuque. "This movie embodies what's great about Iowa, from the kindness of the people to our perseverance."

PIECED TOGETHER:
IOWA BARN QUILTS STAR IN DOCUMENTARY

Rural Iowa is also showcased in the documentary film *Pieced Together*, which debuted in 2016. The stars of the show? Barn quilts.

Barn quilts have been praised as one of the greatest community art projects ever created. They have become a folk art phenomenon in Iowa in the past fifteen years, turning up on not only barns but also mailboxes, gardens, buildings in town and more. Grundy County, Iowa, started a barn quilt project in 2003, followed by Sac County, Iowa, in 2005. Sac County boasted fifty-five barn quilts within two years of the start of the project.

Sac County proves that barn quilts offer an effective way to help save barns, promote rural tourism and boost economic development. "I immediately fell in love with the barn quilt project when I heard about it," said Sue Peyton from Sac County. "Barns, barn quilts and Iowa are such a natural fit."

Creating Rural-Urban Connections

Just as barn quilts spark rural-urban connections, so do other innovative developments, including Iowa's Urban-Ag Academy. Helen Miller, a former state representative (2003–18) from Fort Dodge, founded the Urban-Ag Academy, which brings urban and minority leaders (including policy makers and legislators) together to inform them about agriculture and rural issues. "With the change in the rural-to-urban makeup of the population and their legislative bodies, it is time to create an environment for interactive problem-solving and the exchange of ideas," according to the Urban-Ag Academy.

Miller, an African American woman, could be considered a nontraditional lawmaker from rural Iowa. Born in New Jersey, she received her Juris Doctor degree from the Georgetown University Law Center in Washington, D.C. She often worked closely with the farm community during her tenure as an Iowa lawmaker. "Policy makers, both rural and urban, need to have an opportunity to reach outside their traditional audience to new, fresh faces, conduct educational outreach and collaborate on solutions for mutual concerns," stated the Urban-Ag Academy. "Both rural and urban districts stand to reap enormous benefits from increased understanding of the benefits of agriculture to urban economies and the issues faced by rural constituencies."

Farming Smarter: Tips from a National Outstanding Young Farmer

Another program that helps bridge the rural-urban divide is the National Outstanding Young Farmers (NOYF) organization. NOYF has honored a number of Iowans, including Ben Albright, thirty-eight, a fifth-generation farmer from Lytton. Albright and his wife, Susan, raise corn, soybeans, cattle and cover crops in west-central Iowa. They feed around 2,300 head of cattle annually in the Albright family's two feedlots, farm approximately 1,070 acres and run a Pioneer seed business.

NOYF winners like the Albrights are evaluated on their land stewardship, modern business practices and community involvement. Here are six things Ben Albright has learned about how to succeed in farming:

- DON'T BE AFRAID TO START SMALL. In fifth grade, Albright opened a checking account and took out a loan cosigned by his dad so he could buy a few pigs of his own. "I still remember how proud I was of the pen I built in our barn and the first feeder pigs I raised," Albright said.
- GROW WHERE YOU'RE PLANTED. After Albright's younger brother Nick graduated from Iowa State University (ISU) in 2005, the brothers had the opportunity to work for their dad, Alan, and begin their own farming operation. "We started as hourly employees," Albright said. "Farm Credit Services of America gave us a cosigned loan, and we partnered on two pens of cattle with Dad." By 2006, the brothers had purchased a 450-head cattle feedlot, a John Deere 3020 tractor and an Oswald 250 feed-wagon on contract from their father. By 2008, the brothers had ventured into row-crop production by crop sharing 160 acres and cash renting 80 acres owned by their grandparents. They also bought a 20 percent share of a combine. "This was the year when our informal partnership became Albright Brothers Incorporated," said Albright, who noted the business has expanded in the last ten years with a 900-head cattle feedlot, more farm equipment and more farmland.
- TAKE CALCULATED RISKS. In 2015, Albright had the chance to become a Pioneer sales representative and take over the local seed agency. "After much discussion with my brother and family, we decided this was a great way to diversify our operation," said Albright, who formed Albright Seed LLC.
- BE WILLING TO TRY SOMETHING NEW. Water and soil conservation are vital to Albright's farming operation. "We use buffer strips, grassed waterways, Conservation Reserve Program (CRP) windbreaks, no-till, cover crops, settling basins, manure management, nitrogen stabilizers and conservation tillage to limit our impact on the soil and water," Albright said. When a massive drought hit his area in 2012, Albright began experimenting with cover crops to help his soil weather tough conditions. He started with approximately 20 acres of cover crops in 2012 and is now up to 320 acres, including rye and oats for grazing cattle.
- TEACH OTHERS. Albright was involved in a research study for several years to document the economics of cattle grazing

National Outstanding Young Farmer (NOYF) award winner Ben Albright and his wife, Susan, are raising their family (Myla, Aiden and Teddy, shown here left to right) on their farm near Lytton. *Courtesy of Katie Decker.*

cover crops. "This was a successful project, and I've shared the results by hosting a field day and presenting the information at conferences," said Albright, who is currently involved in a new study to see if there are soil health benefits when cattle graze cover crops.

- GIVE BACK. "Living in a small community means there's never a shortage of opportunities to get involved," Albright said. He is a past president and current voting delegate for the Calhoun County Farm Bureau board; an Iowa Farm Bureau Federation (IFBF) Ag Leaders Institute graduate; a Practical Farmers of Iowa member and Soil Health Conference presenter; and a Calhoun County Cattlemen board member. "I wouldn't want to raise my kids anywhere else," said Albright, a father of three young children. "I want to continue improving my farming techniques and be a mentor to help farmers keep conservation in mind while still farming profitably."

THE "BORLAUG CHAIN": CONNECTIONS THROUGH THE GENERATIONS KEEP IOWA AG STRONG

All these stories reflect the solid foundation that has helped Iowa become one of the world's epicenters of agriculture.

"While Iowa is known for its corn and presidential caucus, there's so much more to this great state," said Mike Naig, Iowa's secretary of agriculture. "It's valuable to understand how modern Iowa came into being and why Iowans past and present share a deep connection to the land. Iowa agriculture is amazingly productive, from crops and livestock to manufacturing and renewable energy. Understanding where we've come from can guide modern solutions focused on conservation, water quality and soil health. When we remain rooted in continuous improvement, I'm confident Iowa will remain one of the most productive, innovative agricultural regions in the world."

Perhaps nothing captures this spirit of hope and reflects the essential ties between Iowa agriculture's past, present and future better than the powerful story "The Borlaug Chain," which Cathann Kress, former ISU vice-president for Extension and outreach, shared in an ISU Extension blog post in 2012.

Norman Borlaug was 91 when he was informed he had personally been responsible for saving the lives of two billion people. He was the Iowan who hybridized corn and wheat for arid climates. The Nobel committee, the Fulbright Scholars, and many other experts calculated that Borlaug's work saved over 2 billion people from famine all across the world—and the number is increasing every day. But maybe Borlaug was not the person who saved the 2 billion people.

It might have been a man named Henry Wallace, an Iowan who was vice president of the United States under Franklin Roosevelt, during his third term. Henry Wallace was a former secretary of agriculture. As vice president, he used his power to create a station in Mexico whose sole purpose was to somehow hybridize corn and wheat for arid climates—and he hired a young man named Norman Borlaug to run it. So, while Borlaug won the Nobel Prize, it was really Henry Wallace whose initial act may have been responsible for saving the 2 billion lives.

Maybe though, it wasn't Henry Wallace who should've gotten the credit; maybe it was George Washington Carver who saved the 2 billion lives. What many people don't know about George Washington Carver is that while he was 19 and a student at Iowa State University, he had a dairy sciences professor who allowed his own 6-year-old boy to go on botanical expeditions every weekend with this brilliant student. George Washington Carver took that little boy and gave 6-year-old Henry Wallace a vision about his future and what he could do with plants to help humanity.

Carver developed 266 products from the peanut that we still use today. And then there's the sweet potato. Eighty-eight uses he developed from it. He also wrote an agricultural tract and promoted the idea of what he called a "victory garden" to ease food shortages during the war. But with all the time and effort and years that Carver spent on things like peanuts and sweet potatoes and victory gardens, isn't it amazing that a few afternoons with a 6-year-old boy named Henry Wallace turned out to make that much difference?

But maybe it was actually a farmer from Diamond, Missouri, who saved 2 billion people. The farmer, named Moses Carver, and his wife, Susan, lived in a slave state, but didn't believe in slavery. They were known as "sympathizers." One cold winter night, Quantrill's Raiders [a pro-Confederate gang of Civil War guerrillas] *attacked the Carvers' farm. They burned the barn, shot several people and dragged off a woman named Mary Washington—who refused to let go of her infant son.*

Mary Washington was Susan's best friend, so Moses sent out word immediately, trying to arrange a meeting, trying to do something to get Mary and her baby back. Within a few days, he had the meeting set. On a bitter cold January night, Moses took a black horse and went several hours north to a crossroads in Kansas where he met four of Quantrill's men. Moses traded his only horse for what they threw him in a burlap bag.

There in the freezing dark, with his breath's vapor blowing hard and white from his mouth, Moses brought out of that burlap bag a cold, naked, almost dead baby boy. And he opened up his jacket and he opened up his shirts and placed that baby next to his skin. Moses fastened that child in under his clothes and walked that baby out—talking to that child every step of the way, telling the baby he would take care of him as his own, promising to educate him to honor Mary, his mother, who they knew was already dead.

That was the night that the farmer told the baby he would give him his last name. And that is how Moses and Susan Carver came to raise that little baby, George Washington Carver. So there it is—it was obviously the farmer from Diamond, Missouri, who saved over 2 billion people.

For the truth is, who really knows who it was whose single action saved 2 billion people? How far back could we go? And how far into the future could we go to show how many lives you will touch? There are generations yet unborn, whose very lives will be shifted and shaped by the decisions you make and the actions you take—tonight, and tomorrow, and tomorrow night, and the next day, and the next.

BIBLIOGRAPHY

Bogue, Allan G. *From Prairie to Corn Belt: Farming on the Illinois and Iowa Prairies in the Nineteenth Century.* Ames: Iowa State University Press, 1963.

Collins, Steven, Iris Hemmingson, Dr. Wayne Marty, Linda Mayrose, Mary Reynolds and Richard Ziettlow. *Le Mars, Iowa: A Pictorial History, 1869–2019.* LeMars, IA: City of Le Mars, 2019.

Drache, Hiram. *The Day of the Bonanza: A History of Bonanza Farming in the Red River Valley of the North.* Minneapolis, MN: Hobar Publications, 1964.

Grant, H. Roger, and L. Edward Purcell. *Years of Struggle: The Farm Diaries of Elmer G. Powers, 1931–1936.* Ames: Iowa State University Press, 1976.

Hamilton, Carl. *Pure Nostalgia: Memories of Early Iowa.* Ames: Iowa State University Press, 1979.

Harnack, Curtis. *Gentlemen of the Prairie: Victorians in Pioneer Iowa.* Iowa City: University of Iowa Press, 1985.

Host, Sandra Kessler. *Adams Ranch Story, 1872–1964.* Omaha, NE: Standard Printing Company, 2019.

Hunter, Rebecca, and Dale Wolicki. *Sears-Roebuck Book of Barns: A Reprint of the 1919 Catalog.* Elgin, IL: self-published, 2005.

Kenkel, Steve. *Kernels of Corn History.* Shelby County, IA: self-published, 2013.

Photographs and Letters: Some Gordon–Van Tine Barns and What Their Owners Think of Them. N.p.: ForgottenBooks.com, 2018.

Prior, Jean C. *Landforms of Iowa.* Iowa City: University of Iowa Press, 1991.

The Story of a Storm: A History of the Great Tornado at Pomeroy. Chicago: Henry O. Shepard Company, 1893.

Taylor, Henry C. *Tarpleywick: A Century of Iowa Farming.* Ames: Iowa State University Press, 1970.

The Union Historical Company. History of Madison County, Iowa. Des Moines, IA: Union Historical Company, 1879.

Wadsley, Virginia. *Nancy Cantwell Wallace: Victorian Matriarch.* Des Moines, IA: Christian Printers Inc., 2016.

ABOUT THE AUTHOR

I f you enjoy fascinating, true stories well told, you have a lot in common with Darcy (Dougherty) Maulsby, Iowa's Storyteller. Maulsby is proud to be part of a farm family that operates a Century Farm in Calhoun County, Iowa, near Lake City and Yetter. She also runs her own marketing/communications company, Darcy Maulsby & Company, from the "suburbs" of Yetter (population thirty-two), since "everything's better in Yetter!" She helps businesses discover and share their "wow" stories. Capturing this magic helps inspire people to dream bigger, revitalize their rural communities and change the world for the good, one story at a time.

An award-winning author, Maulsby has published five books of nonfiction Iowa history, including *Iowa Agriculture: A History of Farming, Food and Family*; *A Culinary History of Iowa: Sweet Corn, Pork Tenderloins, Maid-Rites and More*; *Calhoun County*; *Dallas County*; and *Iowa's Lost History on the Titanic*. Maulsby is a popular speaker who has addressed thousands of people across Iowa at libraries, schools, museums, 4-H clubs, FFA chapters, civic groups, fairs and other events. She has been featured on the Travel Channel, the INSP television network, Iowa Public Television, Iowa Public Radio, WHO 1040 Radio, the *Washington Post*, *USA Today* and other media outlets.

Maulsby is a past president and current director of the Calhoun County Farm Bureau, president of the Calhoun County Corn Growers and District

Advisory Committee member for the Iowa Soybean Association. She also serves on the Calhoun County Historic Preservation Commission and is the president of the board of Central School Preservation in Lake City. She enjoys reading, cooking, going for Sunday drives in the country, helping her family on the farm and laughing at the antics of her beloved pets, including Maggie the Red Heeler and Lieutenant Dan the Cat. Visit her online at www.darcymaulsby.com.